SECRETS *of the* SECRET PLACE

Keys to Igniting Your
Personal Time with God

Bob Sorge

Oasis House
Lee's Summit, Missouri

Other books by Bob Sorge:
- *GLORY: When Heaven Invades Earth*
- *DEALING WITH THE REJECTION AND PRAISE OF MAN*
- *PAIN, PERPLEXITY, AND PROMOTION: A prophetic interpretation of the book of Job*
- *THE FIRE OF GOD'S LOVE*
- *THE FIRE OF DELAYED ANSWERS*
- *IN HIS FACE: A prophetic call to renewed focus*
- *EXPLORING WORSHIP: A practical guide to praise and worship*
- *Exploring Worship WORKBOOK & DISCUSSION GUIDE*

SECRETS OF THE SECRET PLACE
Copyright © 2001 by Bob Sorge
Published by Oasis House
P.O. Box 127
Greenwood, Missouri 64034-0127

www.oasishouse.net

All Scripture quotations are from the New King James Version of the Bible. Copyright © 1979, 1980, 1982, Thomas Nelson Inc., Publisher. Used by permission.

Edited by Edie Veach.

Printed in the United States of America
International Standard Book Number: 0-9704791-0-7

   Library of Congress Cataloging-in-Publication Data

Sorge, Bob.
   Secrets of the secret place / Bob Sorge.
      p.cm.
   ISBN 0-9704791-0-7 (pbk.)
      1. Prayer — Christianity — Meditations. I. Title.

  BV210.3 S67 2001
  242'.2 — dc21   2001035441

Bob Sorge's life proclaims the message of how one pursues and enjoys intimacy with God. His deep experience of God through His word along with his patient endurance of hardship have resulted in "living understanding" of the subject of this book. We do not need more books on intimacy with God but better books on it. Books that flow out of reality — forged out of revelation and encounter. With this book as a road map, gain fresh vision and inspiration for going forward on a journey wherein the very issues of life are in the balance.

— Mike Bickle

There has never been a generation that needs the secret place more than this one. Bob Sorge gently admonishes us to establish a place, time and incentive to meet regularly with God. This book is an enticement, not a guilt projector. The principles he expounds are timeless, tried and true. I loved the book. It stirred my spirit to want renewed fellowship with my Lord.

— Judson Cornwall

My dear friend Bob Sorge's passion for God and His word reverberates through every line of this wonderful book. If you already have similar passion, this book will stoke the fires and fan the flames. If you have little or no passion, this book will ignite one. So, do yourself a favor and saturate your needy spirit in these combustible truths. You will join the ranks of those who are desperate for an intimate relationship with God, the Lover of our souls, who alone can satisfy and fulfill us.

— Joy Dawson

As I read through selected chapters of this excellent book, I could not help thinking: these are the truths the church must hear. Focused, penetrating, passionate and practical, Bob Sorge goes past informing of God's secret place, he takes us there. This is a book to return to again and again.

— Francis Frangipane

You will be encouraged, lifted, motivated and compelled to spend greater quality time with the Lord. This is a book that reveals the secrets that can carry you higher on the mountain of truth and worship. Bob Sorge, through the years, continues to be one of the leaders who pioneers the advanced training of those who have given their lives to worship and intercession.

— Kent Henry

Everything of God flows out of the secret place. Everything good and lasting — everything that survives the ultimate test is born in the secret place. We can "make it" to heaven with empty hands, but why do that? Why not go instead with crowns to lay at His fee? If we give Him crowns, it will be because we met Jesus daily in the secret place. I recommend *Secrets of the Secret Place* to every hungry, desperate follower of Jesus. You won't be disappointed.

— Floyd McClung

Contents

Part 1: Accepting The Great Invitation

1. The Secret of Saying "Yes" 3
2. The Secret of the Shut door 7
3. The Secret of Listening 10
4. The Secret of Radical Obedience 14
5. The Secret of Rapid Repentance 19
6. The Secret of Sowing 23
7. The Secret of Refuge 26
8. The Secret of Decision Making 30
9. The Secret of No Plan B 34
10. The Secret of Burning 38
11. The Secret of Violence 41
12. The Secret of Humility 46
13. The Secret of Intercession 49
14. The Secret of Watching 52

Part II: Making It Work

15. The Secret of Radiation Therapy 57
16. The Secret of Time 61
17. The Secret of Retreats 65
18. The Secret of Journaling 69

19. The Secret of Meditating 72
20. The Secret of Simultaneous Reading 76
21. The Secret of Praying the Scriptures...................... 80
22. The Secret of Finishing 87
23. The Secret of the Morning 89
24. The Secret of Getting Dressed 93
25. The Secret of Self-Denial 97
26. The Secret of Boredom... 102
27. The Secret of Feeling Attractive To God 105

Part III: Setting A Marathon Pace

28. The Secret of Desperation 113
29. The Secret of Manna Gathering 117
30. The Secret of Enduring 121
31. The Secret of Confinement 125
32. The Secret of Waiting 128
33. The Secret of Tears 132
34. The Secret of Holiness 135
35. The Secret of Buying Gold 140
36. The Secret of Inviting His Gaze 143
37. The Secret of The Cross 147
38. The Secret of Rest.. 152

Part IV: Seeking A Deeper Relationship

39. The Secret of True Riches 157
40. The Secret of Beholding Jesus 160
41. The Secret of Standing... 163
42. The Secret of Bodily Light 167
43. The Secret of Just Loving Him 171
44. The Secret of Being Known 175
45. The Secret of Intimacy First 179
46. The Secret of Bridal Identity................................. 184
47. The Secret of Clinging 190

48. The Secret of Walking With God.............................. 194
49. The Secret of Buying Oil 199
50. The Secret of Constant Supply 203
51. The Secret of Abiding In Christ 208
52. The Secret of Union With God 213

Order Form 219

Part I

Accepting The Great Invitation

Secrets of the Secret Place

Isn't it incredible that the awesome God of the universe has invited us to a breathing, growing relationship with Him! This first section of meditations directs our hearts to some of the foundational truths that will help us establish a meaningful secret place connection with the Lord. You may choose to read one chapter a week, or you may take it at your own pace. Either way, say "yes" to His incredible invitation!

1

The Secret of Saying "Yes"

Chris and DeeAnn Abke were feeling over-whelmed by a looming financial challenge. In desperation, they took some time late one evening—after settling their kids into bed—to pray and seek the Lord's help. As they sat together on their living room couch, making their petitions known to God, suddenly an audible voice began to speak, "If you need help, call 9-1-1. If you need help, call 9-1-1."

They heard the voice say this about four or five times, and then it stopped. Mystified, Chris and DeeAnn just looked at each other.

The voice seemed to be coming from the garage, so they cautiously opened the door and flipped on the garage lights, not sure what they would find. Everything was in its place except for a small toy ambulance, belonging to their son, that lay by itself in the center of the garage floor.

Chris picked up the ambulance, pushed a button next to its emergency lights, and the voice began to speak, "If you need help, call 9-1-1." As they wondered aloud how the toy had activated of its own accord, suddenly the Holy Spirit seemed to nudge Chris with these words, "If you need help, call 9-1-1—Psalm 91:1." Going back to the Scriptures, the verse had an entirely new mean-

3

ing to them as they read it together: "He who dwells in the secret place of the Most High shall abide under the shadow of the Almighty."

Chris and DeeAnn understood this incident to be God's way of directing their hearts to a renewed commitment to that secret place relationship with Him. The inference was that God would direct their steps related to their financial needs as they gave themselves to the intimacy of abiding in the presence of the Almighty.

I share my friends' story with you because I am absolutely convinced the power of heaven is unlocked on earth when we devote ourselves to the secret place of the Most High. Therefore, I have written this book with the singular purpose of stoking the embers of your personal prayer life. I pray that you will say "Yes!" to a daily, fervent pursuit of Jesus in the secret place. *My earnest prayer is that with each devotional you will gain renewed momentum and a holy fascination to pursue the greatest pearl of human existence—a personal, intimate, passionate, living relationship with the glorious Creator of the universe.*

One of the best kept secrets of our faith is the blessedness and joy of cultivating a secret life with God. Imagine the sheer delight of it even now. You're tucked away in a quiet nook; the door is shut; you're curled up in a comfortable position; the living word of God is laid open before you; Jesus Himself stands at your side; the Holy Spirit is gently washing your heart; your love is awakened as you meditate upon the gracious words of His mouth; your spirit is ignited and your mind is renewed; you talk to Him, and He talks to you in the language of intimate friendship.

Ahhh, it doesn't get any better than this!

Hell will do everything in its power to misrepresent and distort the exuberant delight of this dynamic reality; this present world system is strategically designed to squeeze out your time and energy for the secret place; the church usually focuses its best energies on getting saints busy; and there seem to be relatively few believers whose secret life with God is so vibrantly lifegiving that it kindles a contagious desire in others to follow their example.

I connect vicerally with the pain of countless believers who carry the conviction that the secret place is central to an overcoming life but who struggle on a regular basis to maintain the secret place as a daily lifestyle. I know what it's like to live below what the Christian walk could be and yet feel almost powerless to change anything. I've watched myself return persistently to the sources which are no source. For example, when wanting to get revitalized from a draining day, we will look to television, as though its distractions will renew us—only to be left empty for the umpteenth time. Or, we will attend a church service in the hope that the preacher's walk with God will infuse us with fresh energy for the journey. But deep down we know that sermons and teachings, although edifying, can never replace the carrying power we find when we sit at His feet and hear His word for ourselves.

We don't need to add another condemning word to the berating voices we all know so well. What we need, rather, is for our eyes to be lifted to the glorious hope we already carry within. My desire is that I might share some secrets—lessons I've learned mostly by doing it wrong first—to empower you toward the goal of the upward call of God in Christ.

When we learn to dwell in the secret place of the Most High, we are positioning ourselves to discover the key to true kingdom fruitfulness. Reproductive power is unlocked in the shadow of the Almighty! One of the best Bible examples of this truth is found in the life of Cornelius, the first Gentile believer. Cornelius was a devout Gentile who committed himself to the secret place of prayer. His piety is described in the Book of Acts as fourfold: he gave regularly to the poor; he lived a holy lifestyle; he practiced fasting; and he adhered to the secret place of prayer. It was because of those four pursuits that God filled Cornelius and his household with the Holy Spirit and made them the firstfruits of all Gentile believers. It's as though God said, "Cornelius, because of your passionate conviction for the secret place, your life is the kind of example that I can reproduce in the nations. So I'm designating you to be the first Gentile to receive the Holy Spirit, because I'm going to take your devotion to the secret place and export it to every nation on earth!" By making Cornelius the cata- lyst for the redemption of the nations, God was giving a powerful endorsement to Cornelius's priority of cultivating a hidden life with God. The eruption of fruitfulness from his life must have caught even him off guard!

Many of you reading this book have a call to neighborhoods, to cities, and also to nations. As you devote yourself to the secret place with God, He will birth something within you that will spread, in His time, to the four corners of your sphere. It's an awesome secret: *The call of God burning in your breast will be uncontainable and unstoppable as you devote yourself to the fiery passion of intimate communion with the Lover of your soul.*

Won't you join me in pressing forward into new dimensions of kingdom power and glory? The face of Christianity is changed, generation after generation, by those who discover the power of the secret place. I pray that with the reading of every page you will join me in saying "Yes!" to the secret of the centuries.

"What is this secret?" someone might ask.

The secret place *is* the secret!

2

The Secret of the Shut Door

"But you, when you pray, go into your room, and when you have shut your door, pray to your Father who is in the secret place; and your Father who sees in secret will reward you openly" (Matthew 6:6).

Jesus Himself spoke these blessed words. All Scripture is God-breathed, but followers of Jesus always find special delight in giving particular attention the words Jesus Himself gave us. When Jesus taught on prayer, He gave primary emphasis to the secret place. In fact, the first thing He taught concerning prayer was the primacy of the secret place. In the verses following, He would teach us *how* to pray, but first He teaches *where* to pray.

Matthew 6:6 contains a powerful secret regarding the *where* of prayer, but before I share it let me ask a question. Do you struggle frequently with feeling disconnected from God? Do you strain to feel God's presence when you pray? Does He seem distant to you? Do you long to know that He is with you, right now, drawing near to you?

If your answer to any of those questions is, "Yes," then I have some wonderful news for you. There is a guaranteed way to get

7

into God's presence. There is a sure-fire 100% guaranteed way to have instant intimacy with the Father, and Jesus Himself gave us the key. Jesus gave us this secret in the above verse when He said, "Your Father who is in the secret place." Jesus is saying, "Your Father is already in the secret place. He has gone ahead of you; He is waiting for you. The moment you get to the secret place, you are in the immediate presence of your Father."

Jesus affirmed this truth twice in the same chapter. He says it the second time in Matthew 6:18, "'So that you do not appear to men to be fasting, but to *your Father who is in the secret place*; and your Father who sees in secret will reward you openly.'" Jesus says it twice for emphasis, so we know this word is absolutely certain. *Our Father is in the secret place!*

Furthermore, Jesus gives us the key to finding this secret place. If you're wondering what you must do to place yourself in the secret place, Jesus made it clear. To get there, all you have to do is *shut your door!*

When you enter your room, and *shut your door*, you are in the presence of your Father. Instantaneously! It matters not how you feel. Regardless of your soul's climate at that moment, you know with absolute confidence you have stepped into the chamber of your Father in heaven. *The secret place is your portal to the throne, the place where you taste of heaven itself.* Receive this word and you have gained one of the greatest secrets to intimacy with God. Because when you *know* you are in the immediate presence of your Father, your spirit and soul will often respond to that knowledge with heartfelt connectedness. The knowledge of this truth will set your spirit free to soar.

When you build your life on the blessed intimacy of a secret place relationship with God, you are building on the rock. You're getting your foundations in order. That's not simply my opinion, that's the explicit teaching of our Lord Jesus Christ. The principles Jesus gave in Chapters 5-7 of Matthew's Gospel were all given at one time, in one great sermon. Jesus said that in this sermon He was laying forth the foundation stones of a disciple's life. Here's how He expressed it:

"Therefore whoever hears these sayings of Mine, and does them, I will liken him to a wise man who built his house on the rock: and the rain descended, the floods came, and the winds blew and beat on that house; and it did not fall, for it was founded on the rock. But everyone who hears these sayings of Mine, and does not do them, will be like a foolish man who built his house on the sand: and the rain descended, the floods came, and the winds blew and beat on that house; and it fell. And great was its fall" (Matthew 7:24-27).

Jesus' message is unmistakable. He is saying, "If you will hear and do what I have taught you in this Sermon on the Mount, you will build foundations into your life that will survive the harshest storms of life." And believe me, friend, storms will most certainly come! There are some storms that have yet to hit your life. The question is, will you have the foundation in place to survive the storms?

One of the most essential elements of that foundation is to have an intact secret life with God. Those who hear this word and do it will not only enjoy intimacy with the Father on a daily basis, but they will also be equipped to sustain the greatest storms—whether they originate from hell's fury or the world's distractions or the floodgates of heaven's blessings.

Don't forget the secret: *shut your door.*

3

The Secret of Listening

When God brought the people of Israel from Egypt, through the Red Sea, to Mount Sinai, He appeared to the nation as a visible fire on the mountain and spoke to them with a thundering audible voice. The experience was so awesome it totally overpowered the Israelites, who asked that Moses go instead and speak to God by himself on their behalf.

The psalmist described this scene with a most unusual phrase: "I answered you in the secret place of thunder" (Psalm 81:7). God viewed the convocation with His people on Mt. Sinai as a "secret place" encounter with His people. He called them aside to a deserted mountain in order to speak with them and give them His commandments.

God has always designed that the secret place be a place where He answers us and speaks to us. Sometimes, He even apprehends us by thundering to us with His awesome voice. There is nothing more glorious in all of life than hearing His voice! God has always longed to have the kind of intimate relationship with His people wherein they hear His voice and respond accordingly. *We close the door to our secret place so that we might shut out all distracting voices and tune our hearts to the one voice which we long to hear.* "The secret place of thunder"—what an awesome description of the place where we come aside to be with our Lord!

Something profound happened inside me the day the Lord showed me the single most important word in the entire Bible. I was on an intense study of Jesus' teachings, and was suddenly struck by how often Jesus talked about the necessity of hearing. For example, He cried out, "'He who has ears to hear, let him hear!'" (Matthew 13:9). His words hit me like a freight train. I realized that everything in the kingdom depends upon whether or not we hear the word of God. The Holy Spirit began to extrapolate that truth for me to the breadth of the entire Bible, and suddenly I saw it: the word "hear" is the most important word in the Bible! The most important treasures in the kingdom are predicated upon the necessity of hearing God. When the Lord gave me this truth, I wanted to underline every occurrence of the word "hear" in my Bible. My paradigm of kingdom living was radically realigned because I was awakened to the fact that everything changes when I hear from God and act upon that word. This is the wellspring of eternal life; this is the fountainhead of kingdom power and authority; this is the source of wisdom, understanding, and life direction! Nothing can replace the confidence and authority that comes from hearing God. *Hearing God's voice has become the singular quest of my heart, the sole pursuit that alone satisfies the great longings of my heart.*

For this reason, I strongly advocate for a prayer life that is comprised mostly of silence. It's a great delight to talk to God, but it's even more thrilling when He talks to us. I've discovered that He has more important things to say than I do. *Things don't change when I talk to God; things change when God talks to me.* When I talk, nothing happens; when God talks, the universe comes into existence. So the power of prayer is found, not in convincing God of my agenda, but in waiting upon him to hear His agenda.

I do not mean to give the impression that hearing God's voice is my daily experience in the secret place. Far from it! Most days I come away with unfulfilled longings, unrequited initiatives, unanswered prayers, unrealized aspirations, deferred hopes, and incomplete understandings. But then along comes one of those days—you know what I mean—when heaven leans over and God speaks a word directly to the heart. He breathes upon a portion of Scripture and personalizes its meaning precisely to my felt needs. Oh what glory! That moment is worth all of the knocking and seeking of the preceding days. I will endure months of silence if He will but speak one creative word from His mouth to my spirit.

My role in the secret place is to listen for anything God might want to speak. If He doesn't speak to me, my time spent in silent listening is not futile or in vain. I haven't missed something or failed to connect. I've done my part. It is so important to me that I put myself in a posture of listening. I'm convinced there have been times I have not clearly heard God's word to my heart because I have not been listening at the time He was speaking. I realize I can't tell God what to speak, or when to speak it. But I can position myself in the secret place so that, when He chooses to speak, I am found listening.

Scripture says, "'Today, if you will hear His voice'" (Psalm 95:7). So hearing the voice of God is largely a matter of the will. We must choose to hear Him. We make the choice by setting aside time to listen quietly. This hearing is a "today" thing that we do. It says "if" because hearing His voice is conditional—built upon the condition of quieting our hearts to listen.

All of us want God to hear our prayers. But the Lord said, "'Therefore it happened, that just as He proclaimed and they would not hear, so they called out and I would not listen'" (Zechariah 7:13). In other words, God is saying, "When I spoke, you didn't listen to Me; therefore, when you speak, I won't listen to you." The inference is that when we hear God's voice, He in turn listens to our voice.

Oh, how can I speak of this wondrous secret more articulately? How can I make it more plain? *Hearing God is the most cherished secret of the secret place.*

Do not believe your adversary's lies. He would tell you that you are unable to hear the voice of God. Nothing could be further from the truth. Jesus said of you, "'My sheep hear My voice, and I know them, and they follow Me'" (John 10:27). You *can* hear the voice of God. Stop everything, come aside, listen, and wait on Him. Wait until. He longs to commune with you.

When listening, it is a common experience to be bombarded with thoughts about all that must be done in our daily duties. A practical suggestion: Take a notepad to the secret place, and write down "things to do" as they interrupt your listening. Then, you can put those thoughts out of mind and maintain your focus where you want it, knowing that you'll not forget about those details later.

Be encouraged by the fact that you're not the only one who finds listening a very challenging discipline to master. The best attainments in God always come the hardest. Be prepared to make the discipline of attentive listening a lifetime pursuit that will become easier in the doing of it. Let's grow together!

The Secret of Radical Obedience

Hearing God in the secret place is one of the greatest keys to the overcoming Christian life. However, it must be linked with its corollary: radical obedience. We hear, and then we do. "But be doers of the word, and not hearers only, deceiving yourselves" (James 1:22).

By "radical obedience," I mean immediate obedience that fulfills the commandment to its fullest measure. *Radical obedience does not seek to comply to the minimal standards but pursues extravagant, lavish fulfillment.* If Jesus says, "Sell all," then we sell *all!* Immediately.

The New Testament word for obedience, *hupakoe*, is a compound word of two Greek words, *hupo*, "under," and *akouo*, "to hear." So to obey is "to hear under." Obedience involves listening attentively with a heart of compliant submission and, then, obeying His word.

Implicit obedience starts, for every one of us, not in doing good works but in sitting at His feet and hearing His word. *Devotion to the secret place is the saint's first great act of obedience.* Jesus revealed this:

14

But He answered them, saying, "Who is My mother, or My brothers?" And He looked around in a circle at those who sat about Him, and said, "Here are My mother and My brothers! For whoever does the will of God is My brother and My sister and mother" (Mark 3:33-35).

The will of God in that moment was for the people to sit at Jesus' feet and hear His word. Until you attend to this responsibility first, you will be constantly frustrated in your inability to uncover the joys of radical obedience. Works of service gain their spiritual energy from the furnace of a fiery love relationship at Jesus' feet. *The true fulfillment of serving Jesus is discovered when we get first things first: First we sit and listen, and then we go and do.*

My friend, Steve Peglow, once told me he thought some people were "common law Christians." By that he meant they want the benefits of living with Jesus without making the commitment. But even as the full joy of living together is found only within the context of the commitment of marriage, so too the joy of following Jesus is found only in abandoning oneself to every word that proceeds from His mouth.

Some people put their best energies into creative thinking. However, God has a way of negating the plans of men: "The Lord brings the counsel of the nations to nothing; He makes the plans of the peoples of no effect. The counsel of the Lord stands forever" (Psalm 33:10-11). Instead of focusing on being creative, focus on being obedient. Give your best energies to waiting on God in His presence, listening for His voice, and then moving out in action only when He has spoken. There's no sense in coming up with your own ideas when it's only God's counsel that will stand! I'm saying it several different ways: The key is in hearing and obeying.

Oh what joy to hear His word and do it! The benefits are profound (I will mention only a few among many):

Obedience unlocks eternally abundant life.

Jesus said, "'And I know that His command is everlasting life'" (John 12:50). Coming from the Master of understatement, these simple words contain far more impact than a cursory reading would reveal. Take that statement to your place of meditation and let Him awaken you to the lifegiving power of extravagant adherence to His command. *The life that resides in Him flows into you when you obey.*

Obedience incurs the gaze of God.

God looks with special interest and affection upon the one who is devoted to obedience. He said it this say, "'But on this one will I look: on him who is poor and of a contrite spirit, and *who trembles at My word*'" (Isaiah 66:2). It's fantastic to just imagine it: You're in the secret place with His word before you, and you're trembling at the prospect of His speaking to you; He sees your willing spirit and conceives of ways to honor your devotion. Wow! To tremble at His word means firstly that we long for Him to speak, and secondly that we tremble with ready diligence to act upon the word that comes. *When we tremble for His word with this kind of keen anticipation, He fastens His gaze upon us in order to do good on our behalf.*

Obedience produces greater intimacy.

In my opinion, one of the most powerful statements Jesus made on earth is right here: "'He who has My commandments and keeps them, it is he who loves Me. And he who loves Me will be loved by My Father, and I will love him and manifest Myself to him'" (John 14:21). *Jesus said obedience is the proof of love, and love brings us into incredible intimacy with the Father.* Furthermore, obedience unlocks the affections of Christ and His self-disclosure to the human heart. There's nothing more I long for than for Jesus to manifest Himself to me! For the hope of beholding Him I will embrace any and every command of His mouth.

16

I choose to obey Him, not because I am energized by watching my obedience change people's lives, but because His presence is so sweet when I obey. My heart is enflamed with zeal for His closeness, and obedience only fuels that fire.

Obedience builds unshakable foundations.

"Therefore whoever hears these sayings of Mine, and does them, I will liken him to a wise man who built his house on the rock: and the rain descended, the floods came, and the winds blew and beat on that house; and it did not fall, for it was founded on the rock. But everyone who hears these sayings of Mine, and does not do them, will be like a foolish man who built his house on the sand: and the rain descended, the floods came, and the winds blew and beat on that house; and it fell. And great was its fall" (Matthew 7:24-27).

You will notice that the storm comes both to those who do Jesus' sayings and those who don't do them. No one is exempt. Storms are most certainly headed your way. The only question is, will you survive? Will your foundations be strong enough to sustain the winds and floods? Those who walk in radical obedience have made themselves ready for the storm, and they will overcome. "'Oh, that you had heeded My commandments! Then your peace would have been like a river, and *your righteousness like the waves of the sea*'" (Isaiah 48:18). The greater the winds that assault the obedient, the more his righteousness rises up like mighty breakers, crashing on the shore in majestic thunderings of fragrance to God.

Of course, there are many other benefits of obedience beyond these four just cited. But I'm trying to keep our chapters in this book short! Consider just two other brief thoughts yet, regarding obedience. The first comes to us through Mary, the mother of Jesus.

Mary gave us one of the greatest summations of obedience: "'What He says to you, do it'" (John 2:5). True servants are found sitting at Jesus' feet ("'Where I am, there My servant will be also,'" John 12:26). Then, when He speaks, they just do it. Servants

17

don't try to give the Master a better idea; servants don't complain that they think the task is stupid; servants don't try to decide if they're in the mood to do it right now; servants don't decide if the task is within their dignity to perform it. They just do it. "'So likewise you, when you have done all those things which you are commanded, say, "We are unprofitable servants. We have done what was our duty to do""" (Luke 17:10).

The closer you get to God, the more obedient you must be. Some choose the level of obedience whereby they endeavor to avoid sin and choose righteousness. That was the level where the children of Israel, who knew God's acts, lived. Moses, however, knew God's ways. So Moses' level of obedience was of necessity much higher. The issue for Moses was no longer simply, "Is this action right or wrong?" The issue was, "What is God's command?" For example, when Moses was on the fiery mountain the command was, "Stay behind the cleft of the rock. Because if you come out from behind the protective rock and see My face, you'll die. You're so close to Me right now, Moses, that if you make a wrong move you'll see My face and have a cardiac arrest on the spot." Now, is there anything wrong or sinful about stepping out from behind a wall of rock? No. But when you're that close to God, it's imperative you follow His instructions to the letter and stay where He's putting you. It bears repeating: *The closer you get to God, the more obedient you must be.*

5

The Secret of Rapid Repentance

Eight times the Scriptures enjoin us, "Take heed to your selves" (Exodus 19:12; Deuteronomy 4:23; 11:16; Jeremiah 17:21; Luke 17:3; 21:34; Acts 5:35; 20:28). Two of those times the words are spoken by Jesus Himself. This taking heed to oneself is a primary function of the secret place. *Prayer is the constant calibration of the soul.* It is a lifestyle of stopping and taking candid spiritual inventory. This is not spiritual paranoia, but rather the exercise of one who has a healthy fear of God and a sublime desire for glorious heights of intimacy with God. The devout is constantly testing himself for spiritual fervor, alertness, faithfulness, purity, love, obedience, growth in grace, etc.

It is in the secret place that I find "my spirit makes diligent search" (Psalm 77:6). I so very much long to please Him and to know His will, so my spirit diligently searches the recesses of my heart to see if there might be anything in me for which I need to repent. I want nothing of my self-life to hinder my relationship with Him or His purposes for us together. I feel like I'm panning for gold—the finds are few and not as weighty as I would desire.

Here's some excellent counsel: *Become a good repenter.* The only way to move forward in God is through repentance. If your pride hinders you from repenting, get over it. You're a wretch.

You need mercy so badly it's scarey. Wise up and master the art of repentance. Call your sin in its worst possible terms. Grovel. Eat dust.

I remember the day I awakened to the reality that I live far below God's glory. I saw it in the story of Jesus' multiplying the loaves and fish for the five thousand: "Then Jesus lifted up His eyes, and seeing a great multitude coming toward Him, He said to Philip, 'Where shall we buy bread, that these may eat?' But this He said to test him, for He Himself knew what He would do" (John 6:5-6). Jesus was testing Philip, to see if Philip was living in the glory zone. Philip would have to live in another dimension to know the answer to the test, which was simply, "Lord, just break open these loaves and fish and multiply them for the multitude." Philip failed the test because his thoughts were a universe below those of Jesus (Isaiah 55:9). Then I saw it so clearly: I am failing the Philip test virtually every day! I am so earthbound in my perspectives that I am almost oblivious to the dimension of glory in which Jesus lives. It's safe to assume that apart from God's grace I am constantly falling short of the excellence of God's glory. Do I need to repent continually? You bet!

Beloved, I pray you might gain the secret of radical, rapid repentance. Ready repentance opens the channels for intimate communion with God. When you're in the secret place, be quick to confess your unbelief and hardness of heart. Don't make Him talk you into it. Agree quickly with Him in the way.

When I speak of repentance in this chapter, I am not thinking of repenting from sins like lying, fornication, stealing, cursing, pornography, hatred, drunkenness, or not tithing. Those sins are so obvious that you don't even need the conviction of the Holy Spirit to know you're in disobedience. God's word regarding those sins is blatantly clear. Sincerity and a clear conscience doesn't even begin until we deal with these kinds of outward sins.

No, I am not talking about obvious sins; in this chapter, I am talking about repenting from our *iniquities*. Iniquities are the hidden faults that we don't see, the wicked residue of our fallen nature that discolors the fabric of our thoughts, motives, feelings, responses, and desires. Iniquities are wrapped up in much

more *subtle* areas of sinfulness, such as pride, rebellion, unbelief, envy, selfishness, ambition, and covetousness.

We all have hidden pockets of iniquity, and we need God's
help to see them. You can't repent of something you don't see, so
God will help you to see them. God has many ways of bringing
our iniquities to the surface where we can see them, and those
ways are summarized under the scriptural metaphor of *fire*. How
God uses fire to surface our iniquities is the subject of this passage:

> "Nevertheless the solid foundation of God stands, having this
> seal: 'The Lord knows those who are His,' and, 'Let everyone
> who names the name of Christ depart from iniquity.' But in a
> great house there are not only vessels of gold and silver, but
> also of wood and clay, some for honor and some for dishonor.
> Therefore if anyone cleanses himself from the latter, he will be
> a vessel for honor, sanctified and useful for the Master, pre-
> pared for every good work" (2 Timothy 2:19-21).

Paul is saying the Christian life is founded on two powerful
realities: We are known by Christ, and we depart from iniquity
when we see it.

*As you are in the secret place and meditating in the word,
God will use the fire of circumstances mixed with the fire of His
word to reveal your hidden faults to you.* As you gaze upon His
perfection and beauty, you will suddenly see yourself in a whole
new light. You will sense His unconditional acceptance despite
your weaknesses, but also His firm commitment to conform you
into the image of Christ. At that moment you are standing at the
threshold of a wonderful opportunity: This is a time to embrace
rapid repentance.

For the devout, this is actually an exciting moment. Repentance becomes the opportunity to turn from things that have
been hindering love, and as such, repentance becomes the catalyst for a greater and more profound intimacy than we've known
to this point with God. When we repent quickly of those things
God's word is revealing, we experience the pleasure of the Father
in a palpable way. The light of His countenance touching our

hearts causes us to actually *feel* His delight in our responsiveness.

As we repent of the iniquities that the fire surfaces, we are actually buying gold in the fire (Revelation 3:18). A consistent pattern of rapid repentance will cause us to become a vessel of gold or silver, useful to the Master for noble purposes. Those who resist repentance do not necessarily lose their salvation, it's just that they do not progress beyond being vessels of wood or clay. They are useful to the Master only for dishonorable purposes (in a great house there is a need even for toilet plungers and dust pans).

The assurance of the above passage is clear: Rapid repentance from iniquity will cause us to progress forward to more noble purposes in God's great house and will deepen our knowing relationship with Him.

6

The Secret of Sowing

Do not be deceived, God is not mocked; for whatever a man sows, that he will also reap. For he who sows to his flesh will of the flesh reap corruption, but he who sows to the Spirit will of the Spirit reap everlasting life. And let us not grow weary while doing good, for in due season we shall reap if we do not lose heart (Galatians 6:7-9).

Perhaps the most common struggle of Christians, when it comes to the secret place, is to feel like they're "spinning their wheels," that their time in prayer and meditation is accomplishing nothing. It's very tempting, in those times of seeming powerlessness, to just move on to something else with a shrug that says, "Well, maybe it will be better tomorrow."

Some of us have become so discouraged with feelings of ineffectiveness that we have fallen into a slump of neglect. I hope the secret of this chapter will help to get you back on track!

Here's the awesome secret of Galatians 6: *When you sow to the Spirit by giving dedicated time to the secret place, you will eventually reap life in the Spirit. Eventually.* We have usually applied this text to the grace of giving financially, but it applies equally to the grace of seeking God in listening meditation. It is

23

impossible to sow to the Spirit without reaping a corresponding harvest.

When I speak of sowing, I am talking about giving of your *time* to the secret place. I am talking about establishing patterns and habits that enable you to spend significant time with God in the secret place on a daily basis. This kind of sowing *will* produce a harvest in your walk with Him. It will change you and, in turn, begin to affect everything around you.

This secret has carried me at times when I was very tempted to give up the intensity of my pursuit of God. When I've been on fasting retreats, for example, I've often been tempted with feeling like my fast is accomplishing nothing in the Spirit. Just when I'm tempted to quit, I remind myself that if I will continue to sow, one day I will reap. I take my focus off my current frustrations and assert my confidence in God's word that a harvest will come my way, in time, if I persevere. I've often experienced the secret of this chapter. Many times I've thought my time in the secret place was rather dull and uneventful, but later perspective showed that it had been, in fact, a powerful time with God. The actual impact of the secret place, I've discovered, is usually not evident until a later time.

We live in a culture that evaluates its priorities based upon immediate results. The voices of the world are demanding that we produce. Now! The race to produce can rob us of investing properly in the secret place. We must not evaluate our spiritual progress based upon how many projects we accomplished or deadlines we met today. Our devotional life with God is more like the planting of a garden. When we arise from sowing into the secret place, we will not usually be able to point to immediate results or benefits. *What we sow today will require an entire season of growth before the results are manifest.*

Sowing is usually extremely mundane, boring, and menial. Rarely are the benefits of sowing seen at the time. Usually, it takes a period of time before the benefits of the sowing start to become self-evident. Authentic spiritual harvest is rarely instantaneous. The wise believer who understands this will devote himself to arduous sowing, knowing that at the right time he will reap if he does not lose heart. "He who tills his land will be satisfied with bread" (Proverbs 12:11). To have a harvest, you must till (prepare) the soil of your heart and then implant God's word into your heart. God's word is powerful seed which will eventually produce a mighty harvest if the soil of our hearts is right.

Every moment you spend in the secret place is an investment. You are investing into eternal realities. God makes note of your labors and considers how He will honor your devotion. And seeds are being planted in your heart that will bring forth a harvest in your own heart—if you continue to persevere in faith and love.

So whatever you do, *don't quit*! When you feel ineffectual, get stubborn and invest even more. The word being sown into your heart today is going to germinate, sprout, send roots downward and branches upward, and produce fruit. *Catch the secret: He who sows will most assuredly reap!*

The Secret of Refuge

There *is* a place of refuge from the storms of life. Storms will unavoidably assault us on this earthly plane, but there *is* a place to hide. I'm referring, of course, to the secret place.

> For in the time of trouble He shall hide me in His pavilion; in the secret place of His tabernacle He shall hide me; He shall set me high upon a rock (Psalm 27:5).

> You shall hide them in the secret place of Your presence from the plots of man; You shall keep them secretly in a pavilion from the strife of tongues (Psalm 31:20).

There is a place where God hides His beloved—in the sanctuary of His presence. Webster's dictionary defines sanctuary as, "A place of refuge; asylum; hence, immunity." God's abode is a sanctuary for the war-weary soldier, a place of immunity from the poachings of the enemy.

David wrote, "So I have looked for You in the sanctuary, to see Your power and Your glory" (Psalm 63:1). The title of Psalm 63 reads, "A Psalm of David when he was in the wilderness of Judah." So my question was, how could David write of looking for God in the sanctuary when he was running for his life from King Saul? He was totally isolated, a political fugitive hiding in the wilderness—and he was there for several years! He had no access to the sanctuary where the ark resided, so he was obviously not speaking of that sanctuary. Any attempt to get near that sanctuary would have cost him his life. So what sanctuary had David found? I believe David was referring to his secret life with God. Even though he couldn't worship before the ark, he discovered the secret place to be a shelter from the swirl of emotions and troubles that constantly bombarded his soul. Here he could vent his anxious thoughts; here he could be renewed in God's love as he gazed on His beauty; here he could be quieted by the assurances of His heavenly Father's protection; here he was healed from the wounds of man's rejection; here he regained strength for the journey; here he was safe.

The secret place is like the eye of a storm. While all is storming about us, we find an inner sanctuary of rest and peace. There's something of a paradox here because we are experiencing both storm and peace simultaneously. When we retreat to the secret place, the storm doesn't stop. In fact, sometimes it seems that when we run into the Lord for help the storm *escalates* in intensity!

Many Christians have been offended by the fact that when they began to devote themselves to the secret place, the warfare around their lives actually accelerated. Instead of finding refuge, they found turbulence. This can be mystifying and so deserves some comment.

While the place of prayer is a place of immunity, it is also one of Satan's favorite places to attack the devout. When seeking to destroy Daniel, the only chink his enemies could find in his armor was his prayer life. So they attacked him in the place of prayer. The only way Judas knew to hand Jesus over to the chief priests was by betraying Him in the place of prayer. So the secret place is both a place of sanctuary and also of the enemy's strategic attacks. The assurance to the believer, however, is that when he is attacked in the place of prayer the Father is exercising sovereign jurisdiction over the entire affair. *Nothing can happen to you in the secret place that He doesn't specifically allow for His higher purposes.* You are totally immune from anything outside His will.

Psalm 91 deals with this tension of safety versus turbulence. The psalm launches with this powerful assurance, "He who dwells in the secret place of the Most High shall abide under the shadow of the Almighty." And we think, "Great! Nothing can touch me there!" But the remainder of the psalm seems to contradict that thought. Verse 3 speaks of being snared by the fowler and being caught by perilous pestilence. (The fact that God delivers us from those things does not negate the reality of the pain we experience when we are initially caught in their grip.) The psalm also describes terrors of the night, arrows that fly by day, pestilence that walks in darkness, and destruction that lays waste at noonday. Verse 15 points to great personal trouble—the comfort being that the Lord will be present in the time of trouble and will bring deliverance. But waiting on God until the deliverance comes can be agonizing at times.

As already stated, some Christians become offended by the increased warfare they encounter when they devote themselves to the secret place. It is this offence that I think may be referred to in Psalm 91:7, "A thousand may fall at your side, and ten thousand at your right hand; but it shall not come near you." Those at your side are your fellow warriors. They get offended that God would allow such calamity to hit their lives after they've been so faithful. Even if a thousand of your comrades fall to calamity and never uncover God's resurrection power—but take God's promises to the grave—it shall not be so with you. Even if ten thousand of your fellow believers are not delivered, He shall be your deliverer. *Psalm 91 must be seen as directed, not at all believers, but at a very specific kind of believer: the one who abides in the secret place of the Almighty.* Thousands of believers may fall to this or that, but it will not come near you because you have learned to abide.

The closer we draw to the Lord in intimacy, the more real the warfare will be we encounter. Francis Frangipane described it with the phrase, "New levels, new devils." As the attacks increase, our cry only intensifies, "Hide me!" While the body and soul may be afflicted with increasing harassment and abuse, the spirit is finding a place of greater protection, rest, and intimacy under the shadow of the Almighty (see 2 Corinthians 4:8-11). The Spirit thus draws us into a place of greater spiritual peace and comfort which only inflames the soul with a greater passion for Jesus— which in turn only feeds the ire of our tormentors.

May you have grace to make the decision now, my friend: lose your life, and pursue the secret place of the Most High. It is the way of the cross. The cross is where we sustain great assaults, but yet there's no safer place in the universe to be.

Oh how I long to direct your heart into this place of refuge! Are winds swirling about your head? Run into the Lord! A refuge is something you *flee into*. A refuge doesn't automatically erect itself around you; you have to seek it out and run into its shelter for safe harbor. As the Scriptures say, "That by two immutable things, in which it is impossible for God to lie, we might have strong consolation, *who have fled for refuge* to lay hold of the hope set before us" (Hebrews 6:18). If God is to be your refuge, you must flee to Him. The cry is, "Oh Lord, I am about to be consumed—I run into You! Hide me!"

"Be my strong refuge, to which I may resort continually" (Psalm 71:3).

Thank You, Lord, for the gift of the secret place!

8

The Secret of Decision Making

Got an important decision before you and not sure what to do? Run into the secret place! Because to God it's not only important what decision you make; it's also important to Him *how* you come to make that decision. It's possible to take the right fork in the road but yet be distant in your heart toward the Lord. Jesus wants you making decisions from the fountainhead of intimacy with Him.

When facing major decisions, Jesus set an example by going to the secret place. For example, He knew it was critically important that He select precisely the right twelve men to be apostles because the right men properly chosen would change the world. So when it was time to choose "the Twelve" from among all those who followed Him, He got alone with His Father in prayer.

Now it came to pass in those days that He went out to the mountain to pray, and continued all night in prayer to God. And when it was day, He called His disciples to Himself; and from them He chose twelve whom He also named apostles: Simon, whom He also named Peter, and Andrew his brother; James and John; Philip and Bartholomew; Matthew and Thomas; James the son of Alphaeus, and Simon called the Zealot; Judas the son of James, and Judas Iscariot who also became a traitor (Luke 6:12-16).

Even the choice of Judas, His betrayer, was bathed in prayer. In fact, the selection of Judas was *especially* bathed in prayer because Jesus knew in advance that His choosing of Judas would eventuate in Judas' horrible destruction and eternal torment. Such a weighty decision warranted a nightlong session of intense prayer in solitude.

Your "Abba" Father loves you so much, He is deeply interested in every affair of your life and longs to be included in your every decision-making process. He Himself has said so with these words:

> I will instruct you and teach you in the way you should go; I will guide you with My eye. Do not be like the horse or like the mule, which have no understanding, which must be harnessed with bit and bridle, else they will not come near you (Psalm 32:8-9).

The key phrase in these verses is, "Else they will not come near you." The horse and mule, so says the Scripture, must be harnessed with bit and bridle if you are to get them to come close. They do not draw close of their own accord.

The Lord is saying, "I don't want to guide you from a distance. I don't want to have to put a bit in your mouth and jerk you around in order to get your attention and get you on course. I want you to draw close to Me—scootch up close to my heart—and allow Me to direct your life from a place of intimacy and communion."

Notice the Lord says the horse and mule "have no understanding," and that's why they don't come near. They don't understand that proximity to the Master will incur for them the greatest benefits. A mule constantly wants to go off and wander in its own way, but in so doing the beast becomes totally unprofitable and unfruitful.

31

Some people are mulish. They just don't get it. They pull away (in ignorant independence) from their very source of life and care and feeding. It hasn't penetrated their thick skulls that the smartest place in the universe to be—and to stay—is right next to God. Psalm 14:2 clearly says that the evidence of understanding is that one seeks God. The wisest thing you'll ever do in this life is to draw close to God and to seek Him with all your heart.

When you pursue this intimacy, you will begin to unlock the greatest secrets of life. It's here He guides you with His eye and directs your heart with His heart. Sometimes we tend to make life decisions based upon our appraisal of surrounding circumstances and conditions. However, the Lord doesn't want us getting our direction from looking *outward* but from looking *upward*. He wants us receiving life direction by beholding His beauty, enjoying His majesty and splendor, and then being guided by the gaze of His eye. So much can be communicated in the expressions and focus of the eye! *Gaze upon His mouth until He speaks to you. Look into His eye until His glance directs the way in which you should walk.*

Those who make decisions based upon external data become *thermometers* of society: Their lives reflect the natural forces that shape their destiny. But those who make their decisions based upon what they see in God become *thermostats* of society: They influence their world through the forcefulness of bringing divinely received initiatives to bear upon this earthly sphere.

Intimacy precedes insight. Passion precedes purpose. First comes the secret place, then comes divine guidance. God doesn't simply want to get you on the right path, He wants to enjoy you throughout the journey. He doesn't want you to find His will and then take off running, leaving Him in the dust. God's primary desire for your life is not that you discover His will and walk in it; His primary desire is that you draw near to Him and come to know Him. God wants to be known! And then He desires that from that knowing relationship there come a tender walking together in His purposes.

Pursuing a knowing relationship with God in the secret place is not only the smartest thing you'll ever do, it's also one of the greatest keys to discovering your highest destiny in God. So stop right here. No need to read the next chapter just yet. Set this book down, and find a quiet corner with your Friend. Enjoy!

9

The Secret of No Plan B

One of the greatest secrets to intimacy with God is to come to Him as your only source of help and hope. "Lord, in this situation I have no Plan B—no other options to default to if You don't come through. You are the only one who can help me!" He *loves* it when you look to Him alone for deliverance. And the inverse is also true: His jealousy is kindled when we entertain other saviors.

The Lord scoffed at the idolatry of the children of Israel by pointing to the vain hope that a block of wood offered:

> He cuts down cedars for himself, and takes the cypress and the oak; he secures it for himself among the trees of the forest. He plants a pine, and the rain nourishes it. Then it shall be for a man to burn, for he will take some of it and warm himself; yes, he kindles it and bakes bread; indeed he makes a god and worships it; he makes it a carved image, and falls down to it. He burns half of it in the fire; with this half he eats meat; he roasts a roast, and is satisfied. He even warms himself and says, "Ah! I am warm, I have seen the fire." And the rest of it he makes into a god, his carved image. He falls down before it and worships it, prays to it and says, "Deliver me, for you are my god!"

They do not know nor understand; for He has shut their eyes, so that they cannot see, and their hearts, so that they cannot understand. And no one considers in his heart, nor is there knowledge nor understanding to say, "I have burned half of it in the fire, yes, I have also baked bread on its coals; I have roasted meat and eaten it; and shall I make the rest of it an abomination? Shall I fall down before a block of wood?" He feeds on ashes; a deceived heart has turned him aside; and he cannot deliver his soul, nor say, "Is there not a lie in my right hand?" (Isaiah 44:14-20).

As I was meditating in this passage, the Lord gave me a definition of a false god. This definition helps me because even though in our westernized culture there are very few people who actually worship figures of wood or stone, we too have our own false gods. In the passage, the Lord describes the idolaters as saying to their block of wood, "Deliver me, for you are my god!" So a god is defined as this: *anything to which we ascribe the power to deliver us*.

Westerners have their own set of false gods—sources to which they turn for deliverance when in times of crisis or need (let the reader understand):

- Money
- Health insurance
- Medical treatment/prescriptions
- Social Security
- Retirement plans and IRA's
- Credit cards/consolidation loans
- Drugs/alcohol
- Pleasure/entertainment/recreation/sports
- Sex
- Friends (to deliver us from loneliness)
- Counselors
- Lawsuits
- Filing bankruptcy
- etc.

These other saviors campaign for our allegiance. Everywhere we turn, the gods of our culture are promoting their powers. Television commercials promote the many alternatives for relief: "Try me! Let me heal your pain. I am your answer. Look no further. Come to me, and I will deliver you."

Something dynamic happens in your spirit when you look at some of those sources of deliverance and say, "No! God, You alone are my Deliverer!" Not only is your own spirit tenderized through such singular affection, but the response of the Father in the way He moves upon your heart is quite without parallel.

God-worshipers are those who come to God *first* in their time of need. They seek God's face and wait on Him to receive directives for the course to take. The secret place becomes the threshold where we wait upon God, seeking His powerful intervention, and crying out to Him for wisdom and revelation.

Occasionally, the Spirit will say to you, "In this instance, I want you to wait on Me only and stand in faith until I intervene sovereignly in your situation." When God gives you this word, then *fasten your seatbelt!* You are in for the ride of your life. You are stepping into the God zone. Here we find the stuff of miracles. This is the dimension where God rises up in His wrath and vengeance and wreaks havoc upon your enemies. Your role is to gaze upon Him, love Him, and grow in patience and faith; His role is to loose resurrection power in His time and way. Not every crisis you face falls into this category, but when it does…get excited! You're taking the high road of the greatest saints of history, the pathway where God reveals the power of His arm, the splendor of His majestic beauty, and the awesomeness of His eternal purposes.

It is toward this glorious dimension that David pointed:

My soul, wait silently for God alone, for my expectation is from Him. He only is my rock and my salvation; He is my defense; I shall not be moved. In God is my salvation and my glory; the rock of my strength, and my refuge, is in God. Trust in Him at all times, you people; pour out your heart before Him; God is a refuge for us. Selah (Psalm 62:5-8).

As I write this chapter, I am personally in great need of divine intervention in regard to a physical infirmity. I have been tempted to consider some other avenues of relief, such as those listed above. But instead, I have said to the Lord, "You only are my Helper. If You don't save me, I am not saved. If You don't heal me, I am not healed. If You don't deliver me, I am not delivered. I have no other recourse, no Plan B, no alternative plan. I am not entertaining other options. It's You and You alone. I worship You. You are my God!"

This is the "single eye" to which Jesus pointed. Jesus said, "'If therefore your eye is good, your whole body will be full of light'" (Matthew 6:22). The old King James Version says, "If therefore thine eye be single." Whether translated "good" or "single," the original Greek word means to be void of duplicity, to have singularity of focus. When your eye is focused on God alone as your Savior and Deliverer, you open to the fullness of light He destines to fill your entire being.

This singular focus is what David prayed for: "Teach me Your way, O LORD; I will walk in Your truth; *unite my heart to fear Your name*" (Psalm 86:11). By praying, "Unite my heart," David was saying, "Lord, give me an undivided heart, a single focus that sees only You as the sovereign power to be feared and worshiped."

In my experience, I have found that the Lord will test us to see if we truly own this reality. He will allow a great storm to descend upon our lives for a strategic purpose. Our natural reflex will be to find a source of immediate relief. We tend to explore all our options.

Is it possible, though, that this storm has come to guide you into a higher dimension of kingdom living? Oh, I hope you can learn the secret: When the storm hits, run into the secret place, establish your spirit, and say to Him with unwavering resolve, "You alone are my expectation." Our God loves to prove Himself strong on behalf of those who have no other gods before Him.

10

The Secret of Burning

It's the secret place that lights our fire, that sets us burning. I'm talking about a white-hot, fiery zeal for the face of Jesus and for the concerns of His kingdom. Jesus came to kindle a fire on earth (Luke 12:49) by which He intended to set us ablaze with His very own passions and desires. To maintain its intensity, this fire must be constantly stoked by the intimate passions of the secret place.

You are destined for fire. You will burn for all eternity—the only question is *where*. The longing of your breast is to be a living flame, ignited with the exhilaration of beholding His beauty, worshiping Him with uninhibited abandon, and deployed into the world with self-controlled, calculated zeal that does not love its own life even unto death. You have something to live for because you have something to die for. You long to be a firebrand of holiness, which is why you'll never be satisfied with status quo Christianity.

God's word is a fire (Jeremiah 23:29), and His presence is totally engulfed in fire (Ezekiel 1:4, 27; Daniel 7:9). When you approach God, you are drawing near to the great blazing inferno of the ages. To be set on fire, you must get close to God. *When you feel cold, distant, and "out of it" spiritually, it's time to re-*

treat to the closet, place yourself before the fireplace of His word, and allow the intensity of His face to restore your fervency. The secret to staying ablaze for Jesus is not in responding to altar calls (as good as those are); it's not in having someone lay hands on you and pray for you (as valid as that is); it's not in listening to a good teaching tape or the latest worship CD; the only sure source for staying white-hot is in devoting yourself consistently to the place-of-the-shut-door. It's the place where "the spirit of burning" (Isaiah 4:4) ignites your soul as you gaze upon His glory with an unveiled face (2 Corinthians 3:18).

Do you desire a greater compulsion for the secret place? Invite the Burning One, the Holy Spirit, to ignite the eternal flame of His fiery jealousy in your life. The Scripture says, "'The Spirit who dwells in us yearns jealously'" (James 4:5). The agenda of this yearning jealousy is that Christ's bride might be set ablaze with an exclusive and fiery passion for her Beloved. You can pray nothing more dangerously sublime than to say, "Holy Spirit, let Your burning jealousy have its consuming way in my life, until every competing affection and false god is completely burned away and until one raging, all-consuming passion fills my entire being—love for the altogether Lovely One, the Man Christ Jesus!"

The book of Revelation describes the Holy Spirit in this way: "Seven lamps of fire were burning before the throne, which are the seven Spirits of God" (Revelation 4:5). I have asked the Lord that the same might be said of me, that I might be described as "burning before the throne!"

As a man who longs to burn for God, I have looked at Proverbs 6:27-28 differently from the typical approach. Primarily those verses are describing the harmful effects of adultery, but its secondary application is actually descriptive of the secret place with God:

> Can a man take fire to his bosom, and his clothes not be burned? Can one walk on hot coals, and his feet not be seared? (Proverbs 6:27-28).

When you draw close to the fire of God's word, you are actually taking fire into your bosom—and the leprous, filthy clothes of your old life are being burned away. As you step into the fiery presence of His secret place, you are walking on hot coals—and your feet are being seared to walk in the way of holiness and righteousness and obedience. The answer to these questions is, "No! Take the fire of God into your being and everything about your life will be different!" It's impossible to embrace this living fire and not be changed! Oh Lord, I pull Your fire to my bosom with fearful delight.

John the Baptist was a man who burned for God! God took John into the solitude of the wilderness in order to kindle a heavenly fire within him. When he was finally released into ministry, he was a living flame. Notice that in the following verses thrice Jesus asked, "What did you go out to see?"

> As they departed, Jesus began to say to the multitudes concerning John: *"What did you go out into the wilderness to see? A reed shaken by the wind? But what did you go out to see?* A man clothed in soft garments? Indeed, those who wear soft clothing are in kings' houses. *But what did you go out to see?* A prophet? Yes, I say to you, and more than a prophet"* (Matthew 11:7-9).

Jesus testified that the people didn't go to John primarily to *hear* something, but to *see* something. Jesus described John as "'the burning and shining lamp'" (John 5:35). John was a man set on fire from heaven, a man who incubated his love for God through a steadfast commitment to solitude in the secret place, and thus he became a shining lamp for the entire nation to behold. The people came from all over to see this fire. People are always attracted to a great fire.

Do something dangerous. Get alone with God! His "consuming fire" will burn away all from your life, until all that's left is love itself. This is our God, "'Who makes...His ministers a flame of fire'" (Hebrews 1:7). He'll make *you* one, too, if you'll let Him.

40

11

The Secret of Violence

The term "spiritual violence" captures the intensity with which the last days' generation will pursue God. They will seek God with their entire being, denying themselves and throwing off all entangling sins, in order to run the race with passion, purity, and perseverance. "'The kingdom of heaven suffers violence, and the violent take it by force'" (Matthew 11:12).

This is the hour to seek God with violent abandonment! The signs of the times are clear; Christ's return is imminent; we sense an urgency in the Spirit; it's time to awaken from our slumber and chase down the kingdom of God like never before.

Genuine faith seeks God earnestly. "But without faith it is impossible to please Him, for he who comes to God must believe that He is, and that He is a rewarder of those who diligently seek Him" (Hebrews 11:6). True faith understands not only that God exists, but that He rewards us according to the intensity of our pursuit of Him. God chasers reveal their faith by the way they run. *Men and women of faith cannot be distracted or detoured from their objective because they firmly believe that God is going to reward their pursuit.* And they're right!

Spiritual violence begins in the secret place. It all starts with how you apply yourself to the disciplines of prayer—adoration,

41

gazing, fasting, reading, study, meditation, listening, absorption of truth. This is where violence starts. I say "absorption of truth" rather than "memorization" because it's possible to memorize Scripture without it ever penetrating your spirit, changing your lifestyle, and becoming integrated into the language of your dialogue with God and man.

One of the most violent things you'll ever do is wrestle down all the competing elements in your calendar and consistently carve out the time to shut yourself into the secret place. In the busy seasons, it can seem as though a thousand other voices are clamoring for your attention. Which voice will rule, the voice of incompleted tasks or the gentle voice that beckons you to the secret place? *Swing your sword against the encroaching tentacles that seek to overgrow your secret life with God. Get alone with God, O man of violence! Kiss the Son, O woman of violence!*

It will also require violence to provide your body with sufficient rest so that, when you get to the secret place, you're not constantly falling asleep. This is the violence we exercise the evening before so that the next morning is secured. Everybody has his or her turn at falling asleep when alone with God; that's part of our humanity, and God understands it. However, the man of violence and wisdom will enact whatever measures are necessary to be alert and engaged on a regular basis in this the most delightful portion of the day.

It's easy to confuse natural zeal with spiritual violence. Some people display incredible zeal for God—in the way they worship or share their faith or attend Bible studies. But if it's a natural zeal, it's a zeal that lasts only as long as others are watching. When that person is alone with God, the zeal fizzles, and the intense level of activity suddenly collapses. Natural zeal must be exchanged for true spiritual fervency—a zeal that is energized by an inward, holy fire that burns even when no one is looking.

God has given us one discipline which is an extraordinary gift, a powerful tool providentially designed by God to intensify the violence of our pursuit. I am speaking of fasting. Fasting, when combined with prayer, is one of the most direct and efficient ways to attenuate the pace of your race, especially if you're feeling a little sluggish in your spirit.

Oh, what an awesome little gift this fasting thing is! It's probably one of the most under-rated, under-employed, misunderstood gifts of grace. There is no spiritual merit in fasting; it doesn't earn extra points with God. But it does tenderize your spirit, sensitize your hearing, and accelerate the pace of divine flow in and through your life. For those committed to exploring spiritual violence, fasting is a true friend.

Solomon wrote, "Seek [wisdom] as silver, and search for her as for hidden treasures...He stores up sound wisdom for the upright" (Proverbs 2:4, 7). The imagery portrays godly wisdom as hidden treasure stored up deep within a mountain, and to gain this treasure you must go mining fiercely for it. Furthermore, the Scripture says, "He gives wisdom to the wise" (Daniel 2:21). It's not the foolish who get wisdom but the wise. The wise get more wisdom added to their life because they're smart enough to seek God fervently.

Jesus doesn't respond to all believers alike. He responds differently to those who seek more diligently. We see this in the way He handled the Twelve. Peter, James, and John were invited into some of Jesus' most intimate and awesome moments, while the other disciples were not included. The difference, I believe, is that the others held back somewhat in their hearts toward the Lord, while Peter, James, and John pursued Jesus harder. Some of the disciples doubted Jesus, even after the resurrection (Matthew 28:17), and that reservation of spirit robbed them of the greatest levels of intimacy. Those who had more were given more.

I'm writing these things, dear friends, to inspire you toward your Lord. Run after Him! Seek Him with all your heart! As you seek Him harder He'll draw you closer than ever before. *Jesus didn't favor Peter, James, and John because of their personalities or gift mix; He favored them because they favored Him.* "'For the eyes of the LORD run to and fro throughout the whole earth, to show Himself strong on behalf of those whose heart is loyal to Him'" (2 Chronicles 16:9).

The Lord is not a respecter of persons. He rewards equally all those who seek Him fervently—which is why some don't enter into much in God. As He looks upon the moderate zeal with which they seek Him, if He were to give them the power and glory they requested, He would be violating all those who have sought Him with so much more intensity. 1 Corinthians 9:24 reveals that we run our race in the presence of the other saints: "Do you not know that those who run in a race all run, but one receives the prize? Run in such a way that you may obtain it." God honors our race as compared to how others have run throughout church history. (This is the principle of 2 Corinthians 8:8.) Folks, we have some serious competition here. I do not mean that we compare our attainments with one another in a carnal way, but I mean that we allow the swiftness of other runners to inspire us toward greater pursuits in God.

I get inspired when I read the stories of the great Christian runners of history. I was so stirred in my spirit when I read the story of how Francis of Assisi pursued God in his early twenties. One of his companions tells the story of how Francis crawled out of bed after he thought his companion was asleep. He knelt on the floor, and for the better part of the night prayed one single sentence: "My God and my all." Then he caught a little bit of sleep and awoke with the others. Such an intense pace!

I once read of a Chinese prisoner who fasted for 76 days from both food and water, praying for the salvation of his fellow prisoners who abused him the entire time. At the end of the 76 days, he arose in supernatural strength and authority, preached to his cellmates, and all fifteen of them repented on the spot. Wow!

I heard of some Chinese believers who were together on a 21-day fast because they hadn't seen anyone raised from the dead in three weeks, and they thought something was wrong.

And the stories go on an on. Oh, I love to be inspired by the pace of others!

As you read the following, which is a page from John Wesley's diary, you will see a man who allowed nothing to daunt his pursuit of the high calling of God:

Sunday Morning, May 5. Preached in St. Ann's. Was asked not to come back anymore.

Sunday p.m., May 5. Preached at St. John's. Deacons said "Get out and stay out."

Sunday a.m., May 12. Preached at St. Jude's. Can't go back there either.

Sunday p.m., May 12. Preached at St. George's. Kicked out again.

Sunday a.m., May 19. Preached at St. somebody else's. Deacons called special meeting and said I couldn't return.

Sunday p.m., May 19. Preached on the street. Kicked off the street.

Sunday a.m., May 26. Preached in meadow, chased out of meadow as bull was turned loose during the service.

Sunday a.m., June 2. Preached out at the edge of town, kicked off the highway.

Sunday p.m., June 2, afternoon service. Preached in a pasture, 10,000 people came to hear me.

Go after God! No one else can hinder your race. It doesn't matter how other people might not recognize your ministry, pursue God! Choirs of saints are cheering you from the bannisters of heaven. "We finished the course by God's grace," they're crying, "You can, too!"

"Therefore we also, since we are surrounded by so great a cloud of witnesses, let us lay aside every weight, and the sin which so easily ensnares us, and let us run with endurance the race that is set before us" (Hebrews 12:1).

12

The Secret of Humility

Our violent pursuit of God must be wedded to a gentle and humble spirit. Humility is the foundation of all prayer. Humility says, "Lord, I am empty without Your fullness; I am broken without Your wholeness; I am helpless without Your strength; I am clueless without your wisdom. Apart from You I am nothing. I need You! I need You so desperately that I am pouring myself out to You here in the secret place."

Prayerlessness is the first sign of prideful independence. We begin to trim back on our secret time with God when we're feeling great about ourselves, energetic and optimistic about our future, and confident about the path we're taking. It's the first sign that we're getting full of ourselves.

This morning, even before I knew I would be writing this chapter today, I was enjoying the words of Agur, who wrote, "Surely I am more stupid than any man, and do not have the understanding of a man. I neither learned wisdom nor have knowledge of the Holy One" (Proverbs 30:2-3). The wisdom of Agur was in having a proper self-assessment of his own stupidity. Would to God that we all owned that same awareness! It would drive us back to our knees, back to the source of all wisdom, back to "the only wise God." If He alone is wise, where does that place us?

Once you see His greatness and your bankruptcy, there comes great joy in humbling yourself before the Lord. With what delight the elders cast their crowns at the foot of the throne! They take what represents the aggregate compilation of all their achievements and throw it all down at the feet of Him from whom it all proceeded in the first place. He gave it to us that we might give it all back to Him. None of this was our idea, it all started with Him and it all ends with Him. *He is everything, and as we are joined to Him the poverty of our personal identity is lost in the fullness of His eternal greatness.*

David wrote, "O God, my heart is steadfast; I will sing and give praise, even with my glory" (Psalm 108:1). We know He is referring in this verse to his secret place because his term "my heart is steadfast" was always used of his personal commitment to being alone with his God. He abandoned his heart to God, so he said, "with my glory." What was David's glory? It was the sum total of his attainments. David had the glory of a king—wealth, honor, prestige, dignity, splendor, and power. He also had the glory of being a psalmist and a prophet. He took the total of all God had given him and made him, and presented it to God in song and praise. The greater his prestige, the greater the joy he had in surrendering that to the majesty of God. *What a privilege to lay all our life attainments at His feet in profound awareness of His all-surpassing greatness!* The greater I am, the more joy I have in taking that greatness and bowing it before Him. "And the kings of the earth bring their glory and honor into it" (Revelation 21:24).

He dignifies us that we might have something to lay before Him in humility and devotion. *God dignifies us—with sonship, glory, acceptance, royalty, purpose, significance, wealth, honor, salvation, wisdom, revelation, understanding, status, character, holiness, victories—so that we might enjoy the highest privilege of casting it all at His feet.* What a holy privilege is ours, to come into the throneroom of His presence and empty ourselves of all dignity by prostrating ourselves before Him, worshiping Him with our entire being.

The servant of God who owns his nothingness finds no greater joy than searching out ever-increasing ways to humble himself in the presence of the Almighty One. "'And I will be even more undignified than this, and will be humble in my own sight'" (2 Samuel 6:22). Throw yourself at His feet today; He is worthy of the highest praise!

13

The Secret of Intercession

Intercession, one element in our personal prayer life, is what I am choosing to define as "prayer on behalf of needs other than my own." Intercession is the priestly ministry of a go-between, someone who stands between heaven and a need on earth and petitions the Father for breakthrough.

The writer of Hebrews asked the saints to intercede on his behalf: "Pray for us; for we are confident that we have a good conscience, in all things desiring to live honorably. But I especially urge you to do this, that I may be restored to you the sooner" (Hebrews 13:18-19). This passage gives us a powerful secret of prayer: *Intercession accelerates God's purposes in the earth.* The writer realized he was going to be restored to them, but it would happen *sooner* if they would pray for him.

We can actually buy time with our prayers—"Redeeming the time, because the days are evil" (Ephesians 5:16). *When evil is looming we can postpone its coming with our prayers; and when good is delayed, we can accelerate its coming with our prayers.*

There are many things God has purposed for this planet, and they will most certainly happen; the only question is, will they happen in and with and through us? Will we participate? If we don't pray, God's purposes will happen, but they will not happen sooner. They will be delayed.

See here the infinite power of God to accelerate things on earth and bring world events to their culmination. He can wrap this whole thing up whenever He wants to, but He's looking for a generation that refuses to be bypassed—a generation that's so desperate to be included that they're giving themselves to incessant, violent prayer.

One of the most profound ways you can love someone is by praying for them. Intercession does something very powerful in the intercessor: it joins the heart of the intercessor to the heart of the one being prayed for. In intercession, you are investing yourself in another person's life. It's one of the secrets of the secret place. Our intercessory prayers thus become "cords of affection" which bind the hearts of believers to one another, joining the body of Christ together in the greatest of all virtues—love.

It wasn't enough for Paul to be convinced in himself that he loved other saints. He wanted them to be clearly aware of his love for them—"that you might know the love which I have so abundantly for you" (2 Corinthians 2:4). "That our care for you in the sight of God might appear to you" (2 Corinthians 7:12). Therefore, after loving someone enough to intercede for them, why not find a way to assure them of your prayers? When they know you've been praying for them, they will *feel* and *know* your love for them.

The body of Christ doesn't work properly without the members praying for each other. *Prayer is the immunity system of the body of Christ.* Through prayer, we fight off the invasive forces that seek to disease and afflict the body of Christ.

Prayerlessness in the body of Christ is akin to leprosy. I learned some things about leprosy from Paul Brand, a surgeon to lepers. He says that in leprosy the nerves stop functioning properly, no longer sending signals of pain to the brain. Lepers will begin to lose fingers and toes in accidents because they cannot feel pain when they are hurting themselves.

Drawing a spiritual analogy from that, when the church does not feel pain with other suffering believers, it indicates the presence of "spiritual leprosy." The church's nerves are dead. What happens next is the church begins to lose body members.

Pain signals the body to send help to the hurting member. Pain is absolutely necessary for the body to be able to repair itself and heal itself. Thus, pain is a gift. It is crucial that we feel the pain of suffering members in the body so that we can rise to repair and heal as needed. *Intercession is a response to pain.* We cry because we're in pain. Cries of intercession are the vehement cries of believers beseeching heaven on behalf of one another.

As I think of these things, I am reminded of friends who face chronic illnesses and incurable medical problems. Saints in desperate health straits send an urgent message to the body of Christ: "The church is sick. We lack the power to heal this member. Danger! Alert! We must rally, respond, and do everything possible for this member to be healed." The church's response to this kind of tragedy, however, is often one of distance and unfeeling. We really don't feel the pain of the sick member. We have spiritual leprosy.

I wonder at what grace will be released in the church when we begin to identify with the suffering members of the body as though it were we ourselves who were imprisoned. One of the fantastic mysteries of prayer is how God joins together the international house of affection (the church) through the impassioned support of one another in prayer. Prayer is God's gift which empowers the body to edify itself in love. Do our patterns of prayer indicate that we're feeling the pain? May the Lord put a holy alarm in our spirits over the powerlessness of the church, and drive us to our knees in an impassioned pursuit of the overcoming authority Christ died to give us!

The Secret of Watching

Jesus connected prayerfulness with vigilant watching. Twice He told His disciples, "'Watch and pray'" (Mark 13:33; 14:38). So there's something about prayer that is wide-eyed, attentive, and on full mental alert. In the secret place, we do not hide from current events like an ostrich burying its head in the sand; rather, we bring our awareness of current events to the searching lamp of the Scriptures and the Spirit of God.

Jesus' exhortations to watch were especially connected to His return to earth.

> "But of that day and hour no one knows, not even the angels in heaven, nor the Son, but only the Father. Take heed, *watch* and pray; for you do not know when the time is. It is like a man going to a far country, who left his house and gave authority to his servants, and to each his work, and commanded the door-keeper to watch. *Watch* therefore, for you do not know when the master of the house is coming—in the evening, at midnight, at the crowing of the rooster, or in the morning—lest, coming suddenly, he find you sleeping. And what I say to you, I say to all: *Watch!*" (Mark 13:32-37).

Without a doubt, this is one of Jesus' most gripping and urgent exhortations. He couldn't have made His message clearer. He was heralding believers of all time to constant, vigilant, bright-eyed alertness. And the focus of our alertness is that we be found watching when our Lord returns.

One pastor was asked how many people come to his church. He replied, "Oh, we sleep 800." Sadly, far too many believers are asleep in this the most momentous hour of human history.

The Lord never placed on us the burden of seeing into the future. He does call us, though, to be alert to the hour in which we live and to discern the signs of our times. He expects us to have understanding and awareness concerning *today*.

I know of only one way to fulfill this urgent mandate: through attentive application to the secret place. It's in the secret place that:

- We sharpen our spiritual senses to heaven's promptings;
- We interpret current events through the lens of God's word;
- We make note of those portions and themes of Scripture which the Spirit has been currently surfacing;
- We constantly calibrate our souls and minds to the straight ways of the Lord;
- We quiet our hearts long enough to listen;
- We gaze with rapt attention upon the throne of God;
- We throw off all spiritual sleepiness by being ignited and renewed in love.

One of the important words of this hour is the word "discernment." Jesus wants us to be alert and able to discern the signs of the times. Discernment will be cultivated, not by reading the morning newspaper, but by reading God's word. We gain discernment only through the power of the Holy Spirit (Philippians 1:9). Those who stand at attention in the secret place will carry the wisdom to discern the mystery of iniquity and the mystery of godliness in the earth today.

There are times in my secret place when I put everything else aside, such as my reading or requests, and just pause to ask this question, "Lord, what are You doing in the earth today? What themes are You emphasizing right now? Among which groups of people are You moving in an unusual way? What do You want me to see concerning the day and hour in which I live? What is my role in Your present activities?" Then I wait upon Him for insight and understanding. Oh, how my heart longs to be fully alert and engaged with the things that are on God's heart for this present hour!

"'Behold, I am coming as a thief. Blessed is he who watches'" (Revelation 16:15). When a thief visits, he will often give off small signals of his presence—the turning of a latch, the sound of a footstep, bumping into an unseen object, etc. In a similar way, there well may be subtle signs to Christ's coming which only the alert will notice. Those who watch, if they are attentive, may actually discern the sounds of Christ's coming. What a blessing it would be to be found on active duty and alert at His coming!

> "Let your waist be girded and your lamps burning; and you yourselves be like men who wait for their master, when he will return from the wedding, that when he comes and knocks they may open to him immediately. Blessed are those servants whom the master, when he comes, will find watching. Assuredly, I say to you that he will gird himself and have them sit down to eat, and will come and serve them. And if he should come in the second watch, or come in the third watch, and find them so, blessed are those servants. But know this, that if the master of the house had known what hour the thief would come, he would have watched and not allowed his house to be broken into. Therefore you also be ready, for the Son of Man is coming at an hour you do not expect" (Luke 12:35-40).

The secret place is *the* place to fulfill these words of Christ. There is no replacement or alternative. It's in the garden with your Lord that you gird your waist for immediate action, and that you trim your lamps until they burn with flaming passion. Do not sleep, but watch and pray. It's the great secret to being ready for the imminent return of the Lover of your soul.

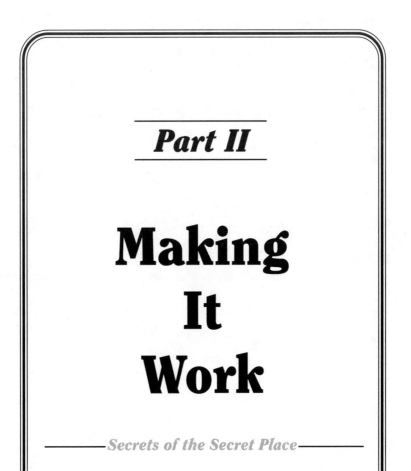

Part II

Making It Work

Secrets of the Secret Place

In Section I, we considered foundational principles to becoming established in the secret place with God. Now, let's look at some practical dynamics—"hands-on nitty-gritty"—that will help us to maximize the potential of the secret place.

15

The Secret of Radiation Therapy

A ll of us struggle to overcome sin. The Bible describes this struggle as "striving against sin" (Hebrews 12:4). Some struggle more than others, partly because their history of worldly living has caused the roots of sin to become more deeply entrenched in their being. Regardless of the intensity of our own personal struggle, each of us has wished at times that we could gain victory more completely over sinful patterns.

The pathway to victory over habitual sins is multifaceted and includes repentance, renouncing of old patterns, prayers of agreement, accountability, forgiveness, self-denial, etc. However, I want to focus in this chapter on one secret to overcoming sin that is sometimes overlooked or forgotten. I call it, "exposing yourself to the radiation of God's presence and word."

Sin is like a cancer; God's presence is like radiation on that cancer. The longer you're in His presence, soaking in His word and basking in His love, the more power you're ingesting into the very fiber of your being.

The only way we change is when we come close to the Lord. His presence is the place of change. *Distancing ourselves from God always produces spiritual regression; proximity to God always produces spiritual progression.* The purpose of the voice of

57

condemnation is to push you away from His presence—that which is the very source of your victory. The purpose of the voice of conviction is to press you into the face of Christ. You can distinguish between conviction and condemnation by considering which direction the voice is goading you—toward or away from the Lord.

God has always longed to draw close to man, but whenever He did, people died. The Law (Genesis to Deuteronomy) unfolds the passionate story of how an altogether holy God with great longings for His people tries to draw close to them, only to face the recurrent frustration of having to kill them for their outright rebellion and transgression. The Old Covenant had a fatal flaw. It required the people to keep their distance because of God's holiness. If they crossed the line, they would die. So many were dying in the wilderness that eventually the people said to Moses, "'Surely we die, we perish, we all perish! Whoever even comes near the tabernacle of the LORD must die. Shall we all utterly die?'" (Numbers 17:12-13). God was also aware of the problem, for He said to them, "'I will not go up in your midst, lest I consume you on the way'" (Exodus 33:3). According to Deuteronomy 5:25-27, the people told Moses they would die if they came close to God, so they asked Moses to draw near to God on their behalf. God's response was, "'They are right in all that they have spoken'" (Deuteronomy 5:28). So God agreed with them and kept His distance. This produced a vicious downward cycle, however. The people had to maintain their distance in order to survive, but their distance from God caused them to deteriorate into further sin—which in turn required that they maintain their distance. This was a hopeless pattern that God had to remedy, and the only solution was the cross of Christ. *Now, through the blood of the cross, sinful man is able to come into the immediate presence of the holy God and subject himself to the glory that will change him.* As we surrender to this glory, we are being changed into the likeness of the glory of Christ! The amazing part is this— that despite our weakness and failure and sinfulness we are now able to come into the immediate presence of the altogether Holy One! What a privilege! Only a fool would neglect or avoid this place of glorious change and delightful intimacy. God has killed Himself (literally) to go out of His way to bring us into His presence.

When we step into the presence of God, we are exposing ourselves to eternally powerful forces. Everything within us changes when we touch the radiating glory that emits from His face. "For the LORD God is a sun" (Psalm 84:11). The sun provides heat, light, energy, and ultraviolet rays—radiation. *When we place ourselves in the sun of His countenance, the radiation of His glory does violence to those cancerous iniquities that we often feel helpless to fully overcome.* Time in His presence is perhaps the most potent procedure to deal with the chronic sin issues that plague us.

You don't know you're being exposed to radiation when it first happens. People who get sun-burned don't realize they've been exposed to excessive radiation until after the damage is done. The effects of radiation are always delayed. The same is true of God's glory. When you spend time in His presence, your first thought is, "This isn't accomplishing anything." However, if you will believe the truth and just devote yourself to mega-amounts of time in His presence, the effects of spending time with Him will eventually manifest.

I have experienced this first-hand, and I would to God that you would hear and believe what I'm telling you. Powerful things happen inside when you spend time with God. *When you're in His presence for extended periods, the molecular composition of your soul gets restructured.* You start to think differently, and you don't even know why. You start to have different passions and interests, and you don't even know why. God is changing you on the inside in ways you can't cognitively analyze. All you know is, sinful affections that once pulled at your soul no longer have their former power over you. The secret is simply this: large chunks of time in God's presence—loving Him and imbibing His word.

One last thought and this chapter is done. When Moses was on the mountain with God for eighty days, in the immediacy of God's fiery glory, the only reasonable explanation for his not dying from the radiation exposure is to suggest that God still withheld from Moses the full strength of His glory. However, the story would also suggest that God helped Moses to "build up" an ability to sustain such a tremendous exposure of glory. The principle is this: *The more time you spend in His presence, the greater your tolerance becomes for even greater manifestations of radiance and glory.* Could we say that you begin to develop a Sontan? Those who expose themselves to large quantities of the radiation of God's glory become candidates for even greater glory. "From glory to glory."

Makes you want to run into the secret place, doesn't it?!

16

The Secret of Time

A friend recently told me, "The secret place has been the point of greatest frustration and attack in my personal walk." I know he's not alone. Since the secret place holds the keys to authentic kingdom overcoming, the enemy will cause his strongest assaults to bear upon this single point of a Christian's life.

Our enemy will do *anything* to get us to curtail the amount of time we devote to the secret place with God. He will push, distract, harass, incite, oppress, entice, weary, lie, intimidate—whatever it takes. Make no mistake, when you devote yourself to knowing God, all of hell seems to resurrect against you.

The full potential of the secret place with God requires one great overarching element: time. Lots of it. The more exclusive time you devote to Him, the more meaningful the relationship becomes. The principle of 2 Corinthians 9:6 really does apply here, "But this I say: He who sows sparingly will also reap sparingly, and he who sows bountifully will also reap bountifully." The more time that you sow into the secret place, the greater the bounty you will enjoy.

There is a threshold to cross in terms of uncovering the full joy of the secret place. Until you find the threshold, you will find that you're consistently pushing yourself to get into the secret place, as though it's a burden instead of a joy. But once you cross the threshold, the secret place becomes a place of delight that you will gladly prioritize over other competing demands.

How do we find that threshold? By giving much time to the secret place. I never consider time invested in the secret place to be wasteful; and even if it is, I gladly waste it upon my Lord! Even when we feel like we're spinning our wheels spiritually, every hour invested is a filling up of the vial. One day the vial will be full, and the Lord will take us through the threshold into another dimension of delight and intimacy. But we'll never get there without investing *time*.

Another friend told me she had feelings of guilt over not taking enough time to be with the Lord. This is a very common feeling, but it is seriously misdirected. Feelings of guilt will never motivate anyone to spend more time with God; in actuality, they will discourage you and make you feel like a failure. Guilt has the potential to totally snuff out whatever small flame there presently might be.

Guilt is always founded on satanic lies. Satan wants you to believe that God is ticked with you because you haven't been meeting your daily quota of time with Him. He militates against the truth of God's word which states that our acceptance with God has to do with nothing but faith in Christ. God is very unimpressed with your performance, but He is deeply impressed with Christ's performance. When you put childlike faith in Christ, Christ's performance record is credited to you. Faith in Christ unlocks the Father's heart to you. When you believe on His beloved Son, the Father's heart explodes in affirmation and acceptance and delight—totally independently of your diligence or lack thereof.

God is your greatest fan. As your heavenly Father, He is constantly coaxing you forward into the heights of spiritual victory. When you neglect the secret place, He's not disappointed *in* you, He's disappointed *for* you. He sees the spiritual riches available to you, and His heart breaks when He watches you getting bypassed. He wants you to share in heaven's best, and He looks with wistful longing when you short-change yourself spiritually.

Someone said to me recently, "The greatest lie Satan attacks me with is, 'You deserve a break today!'" Some of Satan's lies are so stupid they're literally ridiculous. *As though time away from the secret place is a break!* It's not a break; it's a loss. You missed drinking deeply of the Spirit's fountain; you missed being washed and cleansed and renewed in His presence; you missed getting fed by the illumination of God's word; you missed taking the time to calm your hectic heart and hear His precious voice; you missed the intimate communion of the secret garden. As the saying goes, "You was robbed."

So instead of feeling guilty, we should feel *ripped off! When circumstances or emotions are successful at robbing your secret place, don't get guilty—get indignant!* Let *lovesickness* arise in your breast. "Oh Lord, I love You so much; I am really upset at the way I've allowed the cares of this life to crowd You out. This has to stop, things have *got* to change. I can't live without You. I'm coming back! I've *got* to have more time with You. You are my very life, my breath. Oh, I love You, Lord!" And then exert spiritual violence to get your priorities back in line.

On a practical note, many of those who have uncovered great joy in their secret life with God have found it necessary to devote a specific portion of the day to meeting with Him. Giving themselves in a disciplined way to a consistent time slot has been very important in finding the higher dimensions of joy and delight. When we relegate the secret place to spontaneity, in retrospect we find that we didn't give it much time. Go with whatever works for you—because the point is to carve out entire chunks of time that we can devote to long and loving meditation on the beauty and splendor of Christ Jesus our Lord.

Here's another practical tip: *Work your way up slowly to spending more time with Him.* If you're doing ten minutes a day right now, make it fifteen or twenty. By adding incrementally you are building your spiritual stamina. I was once with a brother who was wanting to devote himself to prayer and study regarding a specific struggle in his life. I was amazed, however, that after giving himself to the study for a few minutes, he had to quit and move on to something else. He had developed virtually no spiritual stamina. Even a mere half-hour of study and prayer was too much. He had a case of spiritual "Attention Deficit Disorder." It was time, however, for him to mature in God and develop the ability to spend more time in the secret place.

Train for it like an athlete. No athlete expects to run a marathon on his first time out after being sedentary for many months. He knows he's got to build up his endurance. So every day he adds a little bit more until he's at the endurance level he desires. Similarly, you can build your endurance to the point where spending large portions of time with Him becomes the great delight of your heart.

When I think of running this race, I think of Psalm 119:32, "I will run the course of Your commandments, for You shall enlarge my heart." A runner must develop strength of heart. As he pushes himself to run greater distances, or at a faster pace, the ability of the heart to pump life-sustaining blood to the body is enlarged. I have asked the Lord to enlarge my heart that I might run a harder pace of pursuing Him.

We're not finished with this theme yet. So come to the next chapter, I want to talk about a specific way we can plan more time alone with God.

17

The Secret of Retreats

Nothing equals or replaces a daily, consistent secret life with God. *However, prayer retreats can be highly significant in our spiritual journey to augment and complement our daily disciplines.*

Here are just a few of the ways I have found personal prayer retreats to serve me:

- They intensify and accelerate my pursuit of God.
- They refresh and renew my weary spirit.
- They sharpen my responsiveness to receive revelation from God.
- They have been times of receiving divine guidance for specific situations.
- God has honored them by revealing hidden things.
- They have brought clarity into God's ways and works.
- When I have felt "stuck" spiritually, retreats have helped me to cross new thresholds in God.

I am a great advocate of prayer retreats, and in this short chapter I will do my utmost to convince you of the strategic place retreats can hold in moving us forward in grace. My aim is not only to convince you, but to motivate you to fit them into your calendar.

A friend of mine, Kelly Jenness, has the practice of scheduling a prayer retreat once a year. He usually reserves a room at a Christian retreat facility or a hotel, and tries to time it in such a way that he can spend three full days alone with God. Either he selects a long holiday weekend, or he takes a Friday off from his secular job in order to lengthen the weekend. These retreats have become so fruitful in his walk with God that he is completely sold on them. I have watched many other Christians behold his consecration, admire the fruit in his life, but never become so convinced of the significance of his retreats as to adopt the practice themselves. This leaves me sad and not just a little perplexed.

Effective retreats will wisely include four elements: solitude, no entertainment, fasting, and the Gospels.

- Solitude: Group retreats are useful in their own way, but I am talking about something totally different. Get alone. The quieter the better. Get far away from the everyday demands of life. Shut yourself into your room, except for a daily outdoor walk by yourself. At most, one phone call a day. Face the loneliness head-on. You will realize how social interaction has anesthetized your awareness of God. The violent separation from all distractions is vital to maximizing your retreat time.

- No entertainment: This means no TV, videos, radio, newspapers, computer games, magazines, etc. Part of the intensity of the retreat will derive from your refusal to numb the boredom of being with no one else or nothing else but God. You will eventually move past the boredom threshold, but initially the boredom will serve to reveal your true heart to yourself.

- Fasting: Fasting has the dual benefit of freeing you from the distraction of food preparation and consumption, and intensifying your spiritual pursuit by means of the grace released through self-denial. The more austere your fast, the greater the benefit. A water-only fast is more intense than a juice-only fast. On personal retreats, I typically go on a water-only fast, with the exception of receiving the Lord's Supper once a day. (Tip: Prepare wisely by weaning yourself of caffeine before the retreat begins; pack some Tylenol just in case.)

- The Gospels: Let your retreat be filled with meditations in a wide variety of Scriptures, but by all means include and emphasize large portions of readings in the Gospels. Read the red. Let Jesus Himself hold the central place of your heart during these precious moments. By all means bring a means of journaling because the Lord is about to download into your heart at a rate you haven't known in a long time.

You will probably be amazed at how God will honor your commitment to carve a three-day retreat into your busy schedule, especially if it includes the above four elements. To pastors and leaders who enjoy the privilege of having their full-time employment in the work of God, however, I am recommending a step further. By all means, start with a three-day retreat. But work your way up to even more. I would highly commend a seven-day retreat, then a ten or twelve-day retreat. And for some, even more. Here's why.

Chances are that the first one or two days of your retreat will be filled with above-average quantities of sleep. That's okay, you'll need the sleep to be renewed and to clear the cobwebs. By the end of the third day, it's common to feel like, "I'm just now starting to gain some spiritual momentum." And you're right. I've discovered that the real momentum doesn't kick in until the fifth or sixth day. So for those who have the ability to devote larger chunks of time to an annual retreat, I would strongly urge you to experiment with seven or more days in solitude with God.

I am saddened with the awareness that most of you reading this will not believe these words enough to actually do them. But I am writing for those who have ears to hear. If you can receive it, I am truthfully pointing you to one of the greatest secrets of the secret place. Your secret life can be ignited into new levels with

God through the strategic employment of prayer and fasting retreats at planned intervals throughout the journey.

Fasting retreats have made the difference in my spiritual survival. That's why I'm so passionate about this. I stumbled onto this means of grace in an unexpected way, and now I'd like to "sell" all my brothers and sisters on their effectual potential.

Never done it before? That's okay. Just jump into the waters. You have an awesome teacher, the Holy Spirit, Who is with you. He will guide you into all truth. You don't need any man to teach you; the Spirit Himself will teach you and guide you into the kind of pursuit that fits perfectly for you. Grab your annual calendar, and plan it right now in this upcoming year's schedule.

18

The Secret of Journaling

I am fiercely committed to maintaining a spiritual journal, and it's for one all-encompassing reason: *Those who retain what God gives them will be given more.* Jesus said it this way, "'For whoever has, to him more will be given'" (Mark 4:25).

I don't trust my brain. My memory is like a sieve. If I don't write it down, there's a 99% chance that I'll forget it. So when God reveals something valuable to me from His word, I don't trust myself to remember it. I write it down. He was kind enough to enlighten me with His truth, and now I must be a careful steward of that entrustment by retaining it, meditating upon it, and considering how that truth must impact how I live.

I keep a journal for one simple reason: *I am desperate for more!* And I know more won't be given to me unless I have properly managed what He has already given me. The only way I can keep returning to the things He's given me in the past is by writing them down in a journal in such a way that I can refer back to them in the future.

So when I speak of a journal, I'm not talking about a personal diary. I'm not talking about making entries like, "Today, Susan came over to visit. We had breakfast together and then went to the mall." No, I'm talking of something far more consequential and significant. *Make your journal the place where you chronicle the spiritual truths that quicken your spirit while you're in the secret place.* When God feeds you with His manna, write it down. Then, review it later. Keep visiting that truth until it's woven into the fabric of your Christian experience and conduct.

Let's look at the full context of Jesus' words above.

> Then He said to them, "Take heed what you hear. With the same measure you use, it will be measured to you; and to you who hear, more will be given. For whoever has, to him more will be given; but whoever does not have, even what he has will be taken away from him" (Mark 4:24-25).

I was reading these words of Jesus one day while watching a football game on TV, "For whoever has, to him more will be given." So I put it into football lingo: "Whoever receives what is thrown to him will be thrown the ball again." The best receivers will get the most opportunities. *If a receiver keeps dropping the ball, the quarterback will stop throwing to him. In the same way, if we drop what God gives us, He'll stop giving us more.*

The phrase, "with the measure you use," refers to the measure with which we act upon and live out the word that we hear. If we embrace God's word to our hearts with great zeal, endeavoring to not only be a hearer but also a doer of the word, then He will measure out to us further insight with the same degree of diligence.

But the passage also holds a clear warning. If we are negligent with the insights God gives us, He will remove from our lives even that which we thought we had. (He who keeps dropping the ball not only stops receiving more passes, but he gets pulled from the game.) So a journal becomes all the more crucial for me. I am personally convinced that I cannot hold onto what God gives me apart from writing it down. So if I don't faithfully journal and integrate into my life those things God gives me, He will take away from me even that which I do have. Journaling, then, is a vital element in being faithful before God.

I keep a journal because I am aware of my accountability before God. "'For everyone to whom much is given, from him much will be required; and to whom much has been committed, of him they will ask the more'" (Luke 12:48). May I be found faithful of all that God has given me!

Furthermore, I am aware of Matthew 13:12, "'For whoever has, to him more will be given, and he will have abundance.'" Spiritual abundance is not a guarantee to all believers; it is assured only to those who are faithful with what they receive. *So an abundant life in Christ is not passively received, it is aggressively taken.*

Let me tell you a bit about my journal. It is kept in my computer. This works much better for me than a paper journal. After typing my journal entries, I will often categorize them in my computer according to topics or themes. Thus, my journal entries become a portable library inside my laptop, an array of resources on many topics to which I can turn when studying any of those topics. Perhaps you've guessed it already, but I have leaned heavily upon my journal in the writing of this book (and my other books as well).

I have made the vow of the psalmist my personal ambition: "I will not forget Your word" (Psalm 119:16). When He feeds me with insight from His word, I use every thinkable measure to retain that truth in my heart and soul. Here's my secret: I write it down, and then review it every now and then.

19

The Secret of Meditating

"This Book of the Law shall not depart from your mouth, but you shall meditate in it day and night, that you may observe to do according to all that is written in it. For then you will make your way prosperous, and then you will have good success" (Joshua 1:8).

What does it mean to meditate in God's word? It means to slow way down the reading pace, and to contemplate every word and phrase, looking for deeper and fuller meanings. It's through meditation that we unlock the hidden riches of God's word. God's word is like a mountain range with vast pockets of jewels and veins of gold. The secret place is our time to dig. We uncover various layers of rich understanding as we go deeper and deeper, pondering each word, and turning the phrases over and over. I always assume that every verse has more significance to it than I have yet discovered. Meditation is the art of digging out the most that we can from each and every word.

The written word of God is revealed by the Living Word, through the power of the Holy Spirit. "From His mouth come knowledge and understanding" (Proverbs 2:6). The source of illumination is God's mouth. He must speak to us. So as we meditate in His word, we get in the Spirit and then cry from our hearts, "Lord, *talk to me!*" We realize that without His help we will never unlock the riches of His magnificent word.

Each word of Scripture can sustain the intensity of careful questioning. This focused intensity is seen in Psalm 77:6, "I meditate within my heart, and my spirit makes diligent search." As we meditate in the word, our spirit is diligently searching for fresh insights.

There is so much more depth to Scripture than what readily meets the eye at the first reading. Some truths will never be found until you take the time to sit and stare at the text, carefully considering its contents and implications. Apparent contradictions sometimes contain the greatest truths. Some portions have much more than just one application. They actually contain layers of truth that are uncovered almost like the peeling of an onion.

One of the best ways to meditate in God's word is by asking questions of the text. Some of the most commonly asked questions are: Who is the writer, and to whom is he speaking? What does the verse say, and why? What does it mean? Does the verse contain a spiritual principle? How does this truth apply to my life?

In time, you will develop your own personal way of asking questions of the text. One of the most important questions I've come to ask of a verse is: "Why did the Holy Spirit ordain that it be worded this way?" I question why it says it the way it does, why certain phrases were used, and why other words weren't used. When a sentence or phrase appears to make no apparent contribution to the passage, I will gaze upon it to consider why the Holy Spirit included it. When a verse seems to be purposely oblique or mysterious, my curiosity gets aroused. When a verse appears to be blatantly obvious, I become suspicious that there may be depths of truth therein that I could all too easily overlook.

Here are some other ways to ask questions as you meditate.

- **Context:**
  A phrase or verse is almost always understood better by looking carefully at the verses that precede and follow it. How do the previous verses set a brackdrop for this verse? How do the verses following bring clarity and fuller understanding?
- **Word meanings:**
  Some of the words in the original Bible languages of Hebrew and Greek carry more than one possible meaning. What various shades of meaning do the significant words in this verse contain? Will other Bible translations provide alternate meanings? Will Bible reference materials such as a Bible Dictionary or Lexicon give further insight?
- **Cross-references:**
  A Concordance is extremely helpful during times of meditation to consider other verses that contain the same words, phrases, or concepts of the text at hand. Some Bibles are "Reference Editions" with cross-references appearing in vertical columns or footnotes. Where else does this word occur in the Bible, and how does that other verse bring illumination to our text?
- **Repetition:**
  What words deserve extra contemplation because of their recurrence? Can I discover truths the Scriptures may be highlighting by looking for repeated words or concepts?
- **Symbolism:**
  What word pictures are being used? What do the word pictures represent? Are any of the symbols present in the text representative of deeper spiritual realities?

The one who meditates in God's word will slowly transform the inner well from which his soul draws. Jesus said, "'A good man out of the good treasure of his heart brings forth good; and an evil man out of the evil treasure of his heart brings forth evil. For out of the abundance of the heart his mouth speaks'" (Luke 6:45). Because of our sinfulness, all of us have deposits of "evil treasure" within us. But by meditating in the word, we are depositing "good treasure" within our inner being. *The only way to internalize good treasure is by squirreling it away diligently in the secret place of meditation.* Good does displace evil. The deposit of goodness we have absorbed will be evidenced through new patterns of speech and conduct. In a word, we'll be more Christlike.

Once you come alive to the delight of meditating in God's word, you'll become addicted. The secret place will become your favorite place, even moreso in some regards than the congregation of saints, because it's the place where Jesus feeds you personally. In church, you receive insights that have been processed first through another human channel. The sweetest morsels, however, are those which Jesus gives directly to your own heart. When the Holy Spirit custom-fits the word to your life circumstances, the sustaining power of His personalized word has the ability to carry you through great tribulation. This is the true fountain of life!

Proverbs 16:26 describes the process whereby the Lord will get you addicted to His word: "The person who labors, labors for himself, for his hungry mouth drives him on." The Lord starts by feeding you with His word. His word will satiate your appetite like nothing else. But it also kindles an incredible hunger for more. Once you've tasted of how sweet the Lord is, you're ruined for life. You've got to have more! So you will do anything now to receive the words of His mouth. Your hunger skyrockets, and you know there's only one thing that will satisfy. You are driven to the place of meditation by your own hunger. Being with Jesus in the secret place, gazing upon Him in the word, becomes your all-time favorite occupation in life.

> Finally, brethren, whatever things are true, whatever things are noble, whatever things are just, whatever things are pure, whatever things are lovely, whatever things are of good report, if there is any virtue and if there is anything praiseworthy— meditate on these things (Philippians 4:8).

20

The Secret of Simultaneous Reading

Bible reading, done in a spirit of prayerful submission to God, is dramatically life-transforming. God's word has the power to change us! Revelation 1:3 pronounces a blessing upon "he who reads...those things which are written in it." *All you have to do to be blessed is just read the book.* Those who understand this truth are personally committed to daily Bible reading.

Additionally, we are assured that, "All Scripture is given by inspiration of God, and is profitable" (2 Timothy 3:16). In other words, every portion of the Bible is profitable to the reader. No portion of Scripture should be bypassed or overlooked by those who are anxious to be conformed to the image of Christ. He is the Living Word, and His glory is to be found on every page of the Bible.

Therefore, it behooves us to make a point of reading the Bible in its entirety. I have had a practice for many years now of reading through the Bible, and am firmly committed to this practice for one compelling reason: *I want every single portion of God's inspired word to have a chance at my heart.* I don't want a single issue in my soul to remain unmoved because I wasn't careful to expose myself to the full breadth of His wisdom and revelation. I expect God to surprise me with insight from what I might have thought to be the most unlikely portions of His word. *I want the full package, so I read the full package.*

So Bible reading for me is much more than simply the fulfilling of a daily quota. "Whew, I'm finally finished with today's reading; now I can get on with life." No, it's nothing like that for me. Time in the word is the place of change, and I jealousy yearn to expose my heart consisently and routinely to every living, breathing, inspired portion of Scripture.

Someone once said that the most read book of the Bible is Genesis. That's because thousands of people annually adopt a New Year's resolution to read through the Bible, they launch with the book of Genesis, and then they lose all their momentum somewhere between Exodus and Leviticus. I understand what's happening. Many people do not understand the secret that I am about to share with you.

One of the greatest keys to maintaining momentum in your daily Bible reading, in my opinion, is the secret of simultaneous reading. What I mean by that is, instead of reading several chapters in one book of the Bible, read shorter portions in four different Bible books on the same day. Although there are many ways this could be done, let me illustrate by explaining my personal regimen of Bible reading.

I divide my reading into four sections:

- Genesis to Malachi (except for Psalms to Song of Solomon).
- Psalms to Song of Solomon
- Matthew to John
- Acts to Revelation

I mark the places I'm reading with four paper clips. The first paper clip marks my Old Testament reading. Since my hope is to get through the Old Testament books in a year, I divide the number of pages in the Old Testament by the number of days in the year, and come up with how many pages I want to read each day. For my size Bible, if I read four pages a day I will easily read the Old Testament in a year. The next paper clip marks my reading in the Psalms (I average about half a psalm a day.) My third paper clip marks my reading in the Gospels—I read on average two pages in the Gospels each day. The fourth paper clip marks my reading in the Epistles. Since my hope is to get through the New Testament every six months, I have calculated that I need to read two pages in the Epistles each day. (The number of pages you read in each section will depend upon your own personal reading goals.)

Each day I read in all four sections. This provides many benefits, not the least being that the variety keeps me interested and engaged.

The first section, Genesis to Malachi, has some incredibly delightful sections and some harder-to-read sections. By interspersing my O.T. (Old Testament) reading with other portions of the Bible, I don't get bogged down in the tough passages. And every time I read the O.T., I discover something: *The tough passages get just a little bit easier because I am slowly coming to understand them more and more with each reading.* The Lord has an uncanny way of blessing us most unexpectedly just when we think we're in the dreariest passage imaginable.

When I come to the second section, Psalms to Song of Solomon, *my pace of reading slows way down.* These books contain the language of love, so most of my prayer time is spent here as I slowly and luxuriantly wend my way through the prayers and praises of the psalmists. Here is where I give the Lord the unabashed and open affections of my heart.

And I *love* the third section! *It's in the Gospels that I behold my Beloved, my Lord.* I watch how He moves, how He acts, how He talks, how He thinks. My heart aches to know Him better, to truly behold Him through the power of the Holy Spirit. My primary motivation for absorbing myself in the Gospels derives from the words of Jesus, "'If you abide in Me, and My words abide in you, you will ask what you desire, and it shall be done for you'" (John 15:7). By abiding in Him and devoting myself to His words, I am knocking on the door of answered prayer. Here are to be found the keys to kingdom power and authority, a door upon which I knock daily.

And the epistles of section four? They're *awesome*! I never tire of reading how the New Testament authors articulate the wonder, beauty, power, kingdom, cross, grace, and coming judgments of our Lord Jesus Christ. Oh, the Bible is a glorious book, and I just love to read it!

It's the pursuit of Christ in His word that gets me up in the morning. My time in the word is my lifesource and my sanity. This is the place where I receive grace for another day. Yes, I *love* my daily Bible reading!

I hope you're catching this awesome little secret. You'll gain momentum in reading through the Bible by dividing your reading into three or four different sections and reading simultaneously in each section every day.

If you take on this approach, something else will begin to happen. A truth found in section one will appear in your reading that day in section three; a theme from section two will be reinforced in section four. A verse from one section will give freshness, new light, and expanded meaning to a verse in another section. You'll notice certain themes appearing in multiple places of Scripture. And insights will begin to explode within your heart as verses interplay with each other. This is how Scripture interprets Scripture. The vistas of revelation will begin to expand your heart and ignite your passions. Once this starts to happen for you, you're hooked! Over the edge. Gone.

21

The Secret of Praying the Scriptures

The Bible is one massive Prayer Book. Virtually every page contains prayer prompts. As you take time to soak in His word, not only is your meditation sweet, but you find yourself spontaneously expressing your heart back to God in response to the text.

Praying God's word back to Him is powerful for several reasons:

- God's word itself "is living and powerful" (Hebrews 4:12), so when we pray with God's word on our lips, we know we are praying prayers that are living and powerful.
- When the language of our prayers is shaped by the Scriptures, we gain confidence in knowing that we are praying according to the will of God—a confidence that means "we know that we have the petitions that we have asked of Him" (1 John 5:15).
- As we pray God's word back to Him, the language of His word becomes the working language of our daily dialogue with Him. A powerful transformation begins in your soul when your everyday conversation starts to reflect God-

language. Now your tongue is being ignited by the fire of heaven rather than the fire of hell (compare Acts 2:3-4 with James 3:6).

- We are equipped to pray according to the will of God in ways we would not have considered on our own. The word will tip us off to things we can pray, profoundly widening the breadth and diversity of our prayer life.
- Praying the Scriptures adds a dimension of creativity and surprise to our prayer life, which in turns makes prayer much more fascinating and enjoyable.

If you've never prayed the Scriptures, let me try to get you hooked. If you'll go after what I'm about to show you, you will uncover one of the most wonderful secrets in making your secret place relationship with Jesus absolutely delightful and fruitful.

First of all, though, we need to have a proper definition of prayer. Prayer, in the true biblical sense, is the full spectrum of human expressions to God. Prayer is the all-encompassing title to describe the entire gamut of expressions we offer up to God. Therefore, prayer includes praise, thanksgiving, adoration, intercession, worship, supplication, shouts of joy, lifting of hands, bowing, honor, exaltation, intimate affection, repentance, surrender, dancing, mourning, contemplation, spiritual warfare, prophesying, etc. So when the Scriptures begin to prompt your prayers, you can expect your prayers to cover a wide gamut of expressions.

Now let's turn to a portion of Scripture and try this thing out. Let me suggest we start with a psalm because the Psalms are custom-made for this sort of thing, being that they are prayers already. I'm going to arbitrarily choose Psalm 84 (we could choose any of the 150 Psalms). Turn to Psalm 84, and I will give you some suggestions for praying each verse.

Each verse has major words in it that can be springboards for prayer. Choose a key word or a key phrase, and learn to develop that word or thought in prayer before God. Pray those themes to God, calling on other portions of Scripture that come to mind according to the same theme. Take anywhere from one to ten minutes on each verse, and pray the themes of that verse back to the Lord. Try it. Work your way through some of these verses right now; let's get a feel for this thing.

"How lovely is Your tabernacle, O LORD of hosts!" (Psalm 84:1).
- Tell the Lord how many things you find to be lovely about Him.
- Since His tabernacle is your heart, give thanks for the lovely things He has been doing in you.
- His tabernacle is also the congregation of the saints; extol Him for the lovely things He is doing in His people, His bride.
- Worship the Lord as the Captain of the hosts of heaven.

(As an example, I will "pray" that verse onto this page, printing in bold the words from my prayer that are connecting to verse 1: Oh Lord, **how lovely** You are! Wherever You live is **lovely** because *You* are **lovely**! You make everything that surrounds You **lovely**. Oh, how I long to dwell in Your **habitation**, Lord. I just want to be with You, enjoying You, and being made **lovely** by You. I would rather be with You than anywhere else. The panorama of Your **tabernacle** is altogether **lovely** to me, too. I consider the angels, the seraphim, the living creatures, the twenty-four elders, all gathered around Your throne and fixated upon You. Little wonder—You are unsurpassed in beauty and splendor! O **Lord of hosts**, O mighty champion of heaven, O great warrior of glory, I bow before Your majesty and greatness today. With great joy I appear before You. Thank you for the blood of Christ that grants me this boldness to Your throneroom! How eternally blessed I am, here with You. I worship You, O mighty God!)

"My soul longs, yes, even faints for the courts of the LORD; my heart and my flesh cry out for the living God" (Psalm 84:2).
- Express to Him how much you yearn and long for Him. Let Him see the emotions of your soul at this very moment.

- Realize that you stand in the courts of the great King; express to Him that you stand at attention before Him, totally available to Him.
- With all your heart and also, literally, with your flesh, cry out to the living God.

(As another example, here's my prayer just now from verse 2, with the words in boldface that are triggering my prayer: Oh how I **yearn** for You, my God! Every part of my entire being **longs** for You. I **long** for You with my **soul**, my mind, my emotions, my body, my spirit, my **heart**, my **flesh**, my everything! I want You more than anything else in all of creation. If I can just have You, Lord, You will be my exceeding great reward. If You don't reveal Yourself to me I'm going to **faint** with **longing**. I am so lovesick for You that I am **faint** from love. Oh how I **long** for You! I desire Your **courts** because that's where You live. I just want to live where You live, for the rest of eternity. So here I stand, **crying** out to You, my God. Will You look upon my **cry**? Will You behold my tears? Will you consider the travail of my **soul**? Will You have mercy on me? You are the only God, the true and **living God**, and to You alone my soul rises. Oh, when will You come to me?)

"Even the sparrow has found a home, and the swallow a nest for herself, where she may lay her young—even Your altars, O LORD of hosts, my King and my God" (Psalm 84:3).
- Tell Him how much you want to be with Him, continually—to the point of being envious of a bird that can make its home in the altars of God.
- Tell Him that your heart finds its home in Him.
- Worship Him as your King.

(I'm not going to write out any more examples of my own prayers, I'm sure you get the idea. Express your own heart to your God based upon the words of verse 3.)

Blessed are those who dwell in Your house; they will still be praising You. Selah" (Psalm 84:4).

- Thank Him for the blessing under which you live, because you live continually in His presence.
- Articulate the purpose of your heart to continually offer up sacrifices of praise to Him. It's not just something you do; it's who you are.
- Take some "Selah" moments to praise Him freely and spontaneously.

"Blessed is the man whose strength is in You, whose heart is set on pilgrimage" (Psalm 84:5).
- Remind Him of how weak you are and how dependent you are upon Him for every ounce of strength.
- Tell Him again that you're a pilgrim; you're just passing through this land, in search of a heavenly city whose maker is God.
- Thank Him for the pathway He's showing you in this pilgrimage. It hasn't always been the path you wanted, but it's been for the good.

"As they pass through the Valley of Baca, they make it a spring; the rain also covers it with pools" (Psalm 84:6).
- Even though they're rarely enjoyable, thank Him for the valleys of life. Tell Him about your present valleys.
- Baca means "Weeping"; allow your heart to flow forth to Him, even unto tears.
- Confess your faith in His leadership, that He is enabling you to turn the darkness of your valley into a place of springs and pools—the key to your valley becoming a garden.

"They go from strength to strength; each one appears before God in Zion" (Psalm 84:7).
- The valley may be a place of weakness, but thank God that He is leading you through the valley to the next mountain of strength.
- Rejoice that God is going to turn the darkness of your valley into a face-to-face encounter with His glory.

84

"O LORD God of hosts, hear my prayer; give ear, O God of Jacob! Selah" (Psalm 84:8).

- Pour out your heart to Him. Tell Him how desperately you long for Him to hear you.
- Worship the God who, even as He was faithful to Jacob, will also be faithful to you. He will defend and save you!
- Recount to the Lord how He defended Jacob, and ask Him for the same blessings.

"O God, behold our shield, and look upon the face of Your anointed" (Psalm 84:9).

- The shield may be a reference to loss of reputation because of unanswered prayers; cry out to God to restore your fortunes and vindicate you.
- Realizing that you have an anointing from above, beseech God to look upon you and have mercy on you.

"For a day in Your courts is better than a thousand. I would rather be a doorkeeper in the house of my God than dwell in the tents of wickedness" (Psalm 84:10).

- This is a great verse to help you express how much you love Him. One day in His outer courts is more delightful and exhilarating than a thousand days elsewhere.
- Tell Him that your heart is not set on high and lofty things; you are happy with just being a doorkeeper for Him.
- Call upon His mercy, that you might live in His presence forever, and never fall back to the ranks of the wicked.

"For the LORD God is a sun and shield; the LORD will give grace and glory; no good thing will He withhold from those who walk uprightly" (Psalm 84:11).

- As your sun, tell Him how He is the light of your life, your radiance, your source of warmth, the one who lights your path.
- Worship your shield—the Lord your protector.
- Receive His grace and glory right now.

- Declare your ownership of the truth of His goodness; He will never withhold His goodness from you because you walk uprightly.
- Tell Him you love Him so much that you labor, in accordance with His grace, to walk uprightly in all things.

"O LORD of hosts, blessed is the man who trusts in You!" (Psalm 84:12).
- Thank Him that this verse describes you!
- Tell Him how much you trust Him.
- Worship the Lord of the warring hosts of heaven, for he is releasing His blessings to you.

As you pray the Scriptures, don't be afraid of repetition. The repetition of meaningful words and phrases works powerfully to lodge them in your spirit, and causes truth to have its full impact in your heart and mind. *We want God's word to enter our hearts, grab our attention with its impact, enlarge and expand our hearts with passionate longing, enter into the fabric of our speech and actions, and bear fruit unto eternal life.*

I hope you exercise yourself in praying the Scriptures until you're sold! Once you come alive to this secret, you will want to take your Bible to every place of prayer. You'll take it to your secret place; you'll take it to your home group; you'll take it to corporate prayer meetings. You'll even find yourself praying the word while driving your car!

What a mighty gift God has given in His word. He has given us a way to bypass the self-centered, human-based, pity-filled praying toward which our souls want to gravitate. We can step into His mind, His thoughts, His expressions, His priorities, and pray according to His will from His word in the power of the Holy Spirit. Awesome!

22

The Secret of Finishing

S ometimes our secret place is interrupted by forces beyond
our control. Emergencies happen. And sometimes the
day's agenda demands we depart in order to fulfill a commitment in our calendar—like going to work.

Occasionally we feel like, "I'm not finished yet! Lord, I want
more time with You! I am definitely going to come back to this
same place with You before this day is over. I need to pick up
where we're leaving off and finish my business with You."

The Lord understands when the demands of life pull us away
from the secret place. He is not condemning or displeased. In
fact, He loves to behold the sincerity of your heart when you hon-
estly wish you could take longer in His presence.

Having made that disclaimer, I want to suggest there is an
element to the secret place some haven't found yet. It's the matter of "finishing" your time with God before moving on to the
affairs of the day.

Each visit to the secret place is an event in itself. Many have
understood the need to "break through"—to keep pressing in
until you cross a threshold in your own spirit, until you find freedom in your heart and a connectedness in your spirit. We've
known there is a "warm-up" time, and then there is a time of

intimacy and interaction. *However, we haven't always understood that the secret place is not always complete without the proper finish and full completion of what God intends.* It's easy to leave before God's done with you.

Here's an interesting verse about Jesus' prayer life: "Now it came to pass, as He was praying in a certain place, when He ceased, that one of His disciples said to Him, 'Lord, teach us to pray, as John also taught his disciples'" (Luke 11:1). There was obviously a point of completion and finish to Jesus' time of prayer because it says, "when He ceased." In a technical sense, we know that Jesus prayed without ceasing; but when it came to His secret place, there came a point of time when He ceased. There came the time of completion. In fact, the New American Standard Bible renders it, "after He had finished."

One of the secrets of the secret place is staying with it until you're finished. The way you know you're finished can feel differently every day, but I would suggest that *the decision of when the time is finished is not primarily yours but God's.* Let God decide when it's over. Give Him the honor of dismissing you.

Solomon gave us these wise words, "Do not be hasty to go from his [the king's] presence" (Ecclesiastes 8:3). If it's true of earthly kings, then it's even more relevant for those who draw near to the presence of the King of kings. Having come into His presence boldly through the blood of Christ, let us not be hasty to leave. Let us stop, wait on Him, minister to Him, and continue in our service before the King until His release comes.

Those who linger in His presence uncover the greatest joys of His presence. The greater dimensions of intimacy do not come quickly. We call on Him, and then He gently begins to draw us into the embrace of unspeakable love.

A "hit-and-run" approach will never do. Go ahead and "test drive" this secret. Don't quit till you're finished. Give yourself to the King until He sends you forth into His harvest. The intimacy of His chambers will ignite your soul, and you will carry His fragrance to a lost world who desperately longs for what you've found.

The Secret of the Morning

DON'T DO IT!

What I mean is, don't skip this chapter. It's tempting to look at the title of this chapter and think, "I'm not even going to go there. I'm not a morning person, and I don't want to read about how the morning is the optimum time for the secret place. I've tried it, and it doesn't work for me. I'm a night person, and that's my best time."

That's *great!* If night is your best time, give God your best! I don't believe everyone's secret life with God is identical. We are highly unique, and the Lord loves the particular spice that comes from the fragrance of your own individuality. So give Him the portion of your day that works best for your personality.

For most of us, the morning represents "our best." It's the time when, for the majority, our minds are clearest and most alert. It can also be the most "valuable" time in the sense that many demands want to grab our attention in the morning. Now, I recognize many of my readers work midnight shifts or keep a variety of waking hours. *Therefore, as I refer to "the morning" in the remainder of this chapter, please understand that I am really referring to the "best" and "most valuable" time of your day.*

89

Some of my friends are night people, but even they have told me that morning is their best time for the secret place. One friend said to me, "I am not a morning person, but early morning is the time that produces the greatest rewards for me."

Another friend said, "I am not a morning person," but then she added, "I noticed that when I have my devotions in the morning His word is more fresh to me and I am more obedient to His word. So I have started to discipline myself to have my quiet time with God in the morning. I notice that I am more equipped to handle what gets thrown at me in the course of the day." However, she also added that she uses the night time for Bible reading.

I've heard from more than one person that it is helpful to them to have a set time and set place for meeting with God. By establishing consistency in both the time and place, they are able to go deeper in their relationship with Christ.

It is supposed by some that when God came to commune with Adam and Eve "in the cool of the day" (Genesis 3:8), it was a reference to the morning. Is the morning God's first choice? It's difficult to be dogmatic. Isaac used the quiet of the evening to meditate with his God (Genesis 24:63). Daniel prayed morning, evening, and mid-day. Both David and our Lord Jesus, however, modelled an early morning secret life with God.

David wrote, "Early will I seek You" (Psalm 63:1). The word "early" means at least three things to me:

- I will seek Him early in life, while I am young;
- I will seek Him early on when problems first surface instead of coming to Him after exhausting all my other options;
- And I will seek Him early in the day.

David also described his secret place with these words: "O God, my heart is steadfast; I will sing and give praise, even with my glory. Awake, lute and harp! I will awaken the dawn" (Psalm 108:1-2). David was resolute—"steadfast" in his heart—about the priority of the secret place. He had a constancy of fervency; his zeal for seeking God was unabated and consistently hot. Even as God's love toward David was steadfast, David's love for God was steadfast. He performed his "daily vows" (Psalm 61:8) by steadfastly committing himself to seeking God in the early morning hours, the time when he would "awaken the dawn."

Jesus also modeled a pattern of rising early to pray. "Now in the morning, having risen a long while before daylight, He went out and departed to a solitary place; and there He prayed" (Mark 1:35). The context of that statement is fascinating. It's referring to Sunday morning; the day before had been an extremely busy Sabbath. He had taught in the synagogue, healed Peter's mother-in-law, visited with the group over dinner, and then after 6:00 p.m. on Saturday evening (at the close of the Sabbath) Jesus was suddenly bombarded with a multitude of people who were swarming Him for a healing touch. Once the Sabbath expired, Jesus was instantly mobbed. He healed their sick and ministered to them, and we're not told how far into the night the meeting went. All we know is that the next morning, rising "a long while before daylight," Jesus took off for the secret place. Could it be that the intensity of the previous evening's ministry gave Him an even greater urgency to be with His Father in the morning? One thing seems clear: It wasn't an especially long night.

Even when His body craved more sleep, Jesus knew His true source of revitalization would not be on His back but on His face. Jesus' commitment to the secret place was profoundly prophesied by David in Psalm 110:3, "In the beauties of holiness, from the womb of the morning, You have the dew of Your youth." *The secret place was Jesus' "womb of the morning." It was the place where life incubated, where creativity germinated, where inspiration gestated, where power perculated.* When Jesus burst forth from this womb of happy holiness, He was revitalized and energized in "the dew of Your youth." He emerged from the secret place feeling young all over again and ready to fulfill the Father's mandate.

Thus, Psalm 110:3 describes the three-fold nature of Jesus' secret place relationship with His Father:

- **Intimacy:**
  "In the beauties of holiness" indicates proximity of presence.
- **Impregnation:**
  "From the womb of the morning" points to procreative power that produces life.
- **Invigoration:**
  "You have the dew of Your youth" speaks of revitalization and renewal of strength.

Jesus experienced this dynamism in His secret life with God, *and you can, too!* Not sure whether to do morning or evening? Why not both? Give Him the firstfruits and and the lastfruits of your day. He deserves our *best!*

The Secret of Getting Dressed

S atan reserves some of his most vehement attacks for that moment when we step into the secret place—because he hates what happens when saints connect with their God. Suddenly our sins, failures, and shortcomings begin to play before our eyes like a technicolor video. Many believers subconsciously avoid the secret place because they don't want to face the barrage of shame and guilt that the enemy typically hits them with in the place of prayer. So one of the first things we must do in the morning is clothe ourselves with the Lord Jesus Christ. When clothed with Christ, no accusation can touch us.

The Scriptures have warned us that it's Satan's style to accuse us "before our God day and night" (Revelation 12:10). He doesn't accuse when we're contemplating compromise; but he does accuse us when we're preparing to come before God. So the first step to overcoming the hurdle of accusation is to realize that it's *par for the course*. The accuser tries to pull this one on all of us. It's an occupational hazard of the secret place.

Satan's accusations function on at least four levels:

- He accuses God to us. Satan will point to the way God is fathering us, and he will say, "Look at how God is treating me!" (His accusations always sound like your own voice and your own thoughts, but they're actually his thoughts interjected into your mind.) "I can't believe God is making me go through all of this. God is a tyrant. There is nothing good about the way He is treating me. How can I possibly trust Him when He is handling me this way? He is not fulfilling His promises to me. I don't think He ever will, either." Satan wants us to adopt an accusatory posture toward God. That's why loving God in the midst of your pain is so powerful spiritually, doing warfare to Satan's schemes.

- He accuses us to God. He tells God, in our hearing, what abysmal failures we are. He recounts all our shortcomings, in technicolor and full detail. He paints us as being an embarrassment to the kingdom of God. God is not fazed in the least by Satan's revilings, but sometimes we are. Sometimes we fear that God might be agreeing with our accuser. We begin to wonder if God is mad at us. If our hearts are not established in grace, we can feel dislodged from the love of God for us.

- He accuses us to each other. He will accuse other saints to me, causing me to doubt their walk with God. If Satan can get me to question the motives of my brothers and sisters, the next step is to convince me they question the same things in me. Thus, he designs to cause breaches of relationship in the body of Christ.

- He accuses us to ourselves. This is what Satan is especially good at. He is an expert at berating us for our sins and weaknesses—especially when we are desiring to draw close to the Lord.

Each one of us will find our own unique way of dealing with the enemy's accusations, but here are some fairly standard means of defusing his lies.

- Confess and repent. Satan's accusations carry a sting because they usually contain a certain fraction of truth. So go ahead, get violent. Confess your sin, call it in its worst terms, and repent of it. *So what* if it's the umpteenth time? I know who I am. I am not a sinner who struggles to love God; I am a lover of God who struggles with sin. I am primarily a lover of God, not a sinner. That is my bottom-line identity. So, I will do violence one more time to any known sin or compromise and confess it freely to God, receiving His forgiveness.

- Get under the blood. Oh, thank God for the blood of Jesus! His atoning blood is altogether powerful, eternally effectual, and it alone has the power to cleanse the defiled conscience. The blood of Christ is my basis for entry into the presence of the King. I come boldly now to the throne of grace because I enter by His blood through the veil of His flesh. I am welcome in the highest courts of glory because of Christ's shed blood!

- Get dressed. What I mean is, put on the full armor of God according to Ephesians 6. As you read this portion of Scripture, I want you to notice that the reason for putting on the armor of God is *so that we might pray*.

Put on the whole armor of God, that you may be able to stand against the wiles of the devil. For we do not wrestle against flesh and blood, but against principalities, against powers, against the rulers of the darkness of this age, against spiritual hosts of wickedness in the heavenly places. Therefore take up the whole armor of God, that you may be able to withstand in the evil day, and having done all, to stand. Stand therefore, having girded your waist with truth, having put on the breastplate of righteousness, and having shod your feet with the preparation of the gospel of peace; above all, taking the shield of faith with which you will be able to quench all the fiery darts of the wicked one. And take the helmet of salvation, and the sword of the Spirit, which is the word of God; praying always with all prayer and supplication in the Spirit, being watchful to this end with all perseverance and supplication for all the saints (Ephesians 6:11-18).

Getting dressed all starts with the belt of truth. The truth of God's word is the thing that will enable you to gird up your waist, to prepare you to run. Satan's assault is comprised of lies and half-truths. Speak the word of truth; win the battle for the truth! Stand with confidence in the truth of who you are in God.

See yourself clothed in His breastplate of righteousness. You are the righteousness of God in Christ! Put on each piece of the armor, one at a time—the shoes of peace, the shield of faith, the helmet of salvation, the sword of the Spirit.

Notice that the passage calls us "to stand." You don't have to go looking for a fight; just step into the secret place and the fight will come to you! Suddenly you're thrown into a wrestling match. This is the time to stand firm. Stand upon the truth, come under the blood, and fight the good fight. Stand firm until the enemy admits defeat and leaves you for a time.

When you put on the armor of God, here's what you're actually doing: you're putting on Christ. "But put on the Lord Jesus Christ, and make no provision for the flesh, to fulfill its lusts" (Romans 13:14). Jesus is your every article of clothing; you are clothed with Christ. When the Father looks at you, He sees Jesus. And you are stunningly attractive to Him! He favors, yes, He even *prefers* you! He is so pleased to have you in His embrace. The secret place is where we celebrate the fact that He killed Himself to win our hearts to Himself.

Our clothing in Christ is now "tender mercies, kindness, humility, meekness, longsuffering,…love" (Colossians 3:12,14). This is how we become clothed in the white garments of Revelation 3:5. Here's the secret: *When we realize we're clothed in the very garments of Christ, our confidence level before God soars to the heavens.* Satan's accusations cannot lodge within us, and they just bounce off our shield of faith. We are accepted by the Father, and now we can enjoy the peaceful dialogue of intimacy with Jesus.

Hit with accusations? Get dressed!

25

The Secret of Self-Denial

Then Jesus said to His disciples, "If anyone desires to come after Me, let him deny himself, and take up his cross, and follow Me" (Matthew 16:24).

S ome might think Jesus is saying, "Since I have to suffer so much to procure your salvation, I want you guys to suffer, too." But Jesus did not intend this as a morbid invitation to pain; He meant it as a glorious invitation to intimacy with Him.

"If you really want to be close to Me," He's telling us, "then let Me give you the key. Deny yourself, take up your cross, and follow Me." It's an invitation to the highest intimacy, but yet we often avoid it because we think the pricetag is too steep. What we haven't understood, though, is what we're buying. It's like someone offering us a brand-new Mercedes for $20, and us bemoaning the fact that they're trying to extract $20 from us! Next to what we're buying, the cost is *nothing*! Similarly, self-denial is such a small price to pay for the incredible delights of loving communion with our Lord.

If you can receive it, here's the secret: *Self-denial can serve as a catalyst to help propel you forward into greater joys of inti-*

97

macy in the secret place. Self-denial and intimacy go hand in hand. Self-denial awakens the flow of life and love in the secret place.

Denying oneself is not the same as taking up one's cross. To take up the cross, at least in one sense, is to crucify the sinful passions of the flesh. The cross has to do with the death of the flesh, the carnal man. Self-denial, however, has to do with good and healthy passions. *Self-denial is the deliberate curtailing of healthy passions and desires for the sake of pursuing Jesus harder.*

To clarify, here's just a sampling of the many ways self-denial can be invoked:

- Fasting from or curtailing intake of food or drink;
- Cutting back on sleep time;
- Bypassing good entertainment;
- Saying no to social invitations/fellowship;
- Lessening time given to recreation/exercise;
- Taking a temporary hiatus from marital relations;
- Accepting a vow of celibacy;
- Spending less when you could afford more;
- Etc.

None of the above activities are sinful. Practiced in moderation and balance, they are gifts of God that we might enjoy a fulfilling and satisfying life. But some people want more than a happy life. They want to know Jesus; they aspire to achieve kingdom conquest; they desire to accrue eternal treasure; they long for the outpouring of God's Spirit in this generation. So they're pressing into the kingdom with spiritual violence. Self-denial is Christ's gift to us that enables us to turn up the furnace of our love seven times hotter.

Some spiritual benefits of self-denial include:

Clearer Perspective
The more you deny yourself, the more the scales fall from your eyes. You will begin to see the world for what it is (we natu-

rally get desensitized to the filth of the world system that sur-rounds us). The world denies itself nothing, so when you em-brace self-denial you are doing something other-worldly. Self-denial demonstrates that we do not love the world nor the things in the world.

It was the lack of food that finally brought the prodigal son to his senses. "But when he came to himself, he said, 'How many of my father's hired servants have bread enough and to spare, and I perish with hunger!'" (Luke 15:17). In a similar way, authentic spiritual fasting is a powerful asset in helping us to re-orient again to true kingdom values and realities.

Accelerated Change

When you begin to see how worldliness has infected your lifestyle, grace is released for embracing personal change. The simple truth is that the Lord Jesus honors self-denial. He loves the passionate resolve and humility of those who willingly em-brace self-denial, so He rewards it with grace to gain personal purity and true holiness. He gives grace to the humble.

In speaking of fasting, Jesus said, "'And no one puts new wine into old wineskins; or else the new wine bursts the wineskins, the wine is spilled, and the wineskins are ruined. But new wine must be put into new wineskins'" (Mark 2:22). Jesus clearly taught that fasting plays a critical role in preparing old wineskins to once again receive new wine. Self-denial has a powerful shaping effect upon the soul, preparing us for the new wine of God's fresh moving among us.

Preparation For Prophetic Ministry

When something is practiced in excess, you cannot have a voice to that while practising it in moderation. To have a voice to the excessive, you must sanctify yourself from even the bal-anced, healthy expression of that practice.

Jesus modelled this principle. To address the greed of the Pharisees, Jesus wouldn't even allow Himself to touch money. To address the tendency of the Pharisees to concentrate on spe-cial garments, Jesus wore a very plain garment. To address their love for the best places at feasts and in the synagogues, Jesus didn't seat Himself with them. *Jesus sanctified Himself from the good and normal in order to have a voice into the excessive and imbalanced.*

Those who carry a prophetic message to the body of Christ usually will embrace self-denial on almost a daily basis. Strategic forms of self-denial qualify us to be stewards of a prophetic message to the body of Christ.

Ability To Hear God

One of the prime benefits of self-denial is the way it empowers us to hear more clearly from God. *Answers, guidance, direction, insight—all seem to flow more freely when self-denial is freely and willingly embraced with grace in the heart.*

Mike Bickle speaks so articulately about fasting being a form of "voluntary weakness." Voluntary weakness, as he uses the term, is the intentional embracing of weakness for the purpose of uncovering greater grace. Self-denial has a weakening effect on the human vessel. It makes us more vulnerable. Those who embrace voluntary weakness have personal ownership of this great principle: "'My grace is sufficient for you, for My strength is made perfect in weakness'" (2 Corinthians 12:9). When we embrace weakness, His grace rushes in to strengthen us. Those who embrace self-denial will be stronger in hearing God's voice and understanding His will.

Jesus connected the secret place intrinsically with self-denial. He said,

> "Moreover, when you fast, do not be like the hypocrites, with a sad countenance. For they disfigure their faces that they may appear to men to be fasting. Assuredly, I say to you, they have their reward. But you, when you fast, anoint your head and wash your face, so that you do not appear to men to be fasting, but to your Father who is in the secret place; and your Father who sees in secret will reward you openly" (Matthew 6:16-18).

Self-denial is practiced in secret. It is done quietly and exclusively for God, to be seen by His eyes alone. When practiced in purity before our loving Father, self-denial serves to awaken the flow of life in the secret place.

Want in on a secret? *When your secret place needs revitalization, embrace the grace of self-denial.* Your heart will be touched more readily, your spirit will soar higher, and your awareness of His presence will increase.

26

The Secret of Boredom

Ever get bored while praying?

If we're to be truthful, *every one of us* has been bored in the secret place. Here's the next little secret that this book is going to reveal with consummate eloquence: *Everybody gets bored in their personal prayer life and Bible reading.* Even the twelve "apostles of the Lamb" fell asleep in the place of prayer (Matthew 26:40-45)!

There are some days when I seem to have an especially good connection with God. On those days I often think, "Why isn't it like this all the time?" But in reality, there are a lot of deadpan days mixed in with the great ones.

Some days I am so looking forward to my time with the Lord, only to sleep right through the entire time. Other times I seem to be awake enough; it's just that there's no wind of the Spirit blowing on this particular day for me. No matter what I read, or how fervently I pray, this one seems destined to be a dud.

And I'm not alone. When I talk with others, I realize this is the common experience of weak human beings who, in their brokenness and frailty, are continually falling short of the kind of connection with God for which their heart yearns. "The spirit indeed is willing, but the flesh is weak" (Jesus spoke those words directly related to prayer, Matthew 26:41).

So, what should we do when we're bored? Do it anyway. Persevere. Do the time. Grind it out. Bite the bullet.

Allow nothing to dissuade or detour you, boredom included. Sometime along the way, we need to make a determined life decision: "I am devoting myself by God's grace to the secret place, come rain or shine, good days or bad days, when I feel like it or when I don't feel like it, when it's easy and when it's hard." When you figure in God's grace, you can do all things through Christ who strengthens you.

The Lord responds to sincere cries of, "Help!" When we are feeling especially weak, that's the time to reach out to Him for the abundance of His grace. "Likewise the Spirit also helps in our weaknesses. For we do not know what we should pray for as we ought, but the Spirit Himself makes intercession for us with groanings which cannot be uttered" (Romans 8:26). Jesus called the Holy Spirit "the Helper" (John 14:16, 26; 15:26; 16:7), because He was given to us to help us in our times of weakness and need. Call on your Helper! "Holy Spirit, I need You right now. Help!" He will come to your aid because He loves to help us pray.

When I fall asleep in the secret place, I don't allow the enemy to use that against me. I just see myself as His little child, curled up in His lap, so at peace with Him that I am resting in childlike simplicity in His arms. I imagine the Lord using that time to gaze upon me and enjoy the warmth of our nearness. I could have fallen asleep elsewhere, but I chose to do it in His arms.

I am writing this chapter primarily to defuse the enemy's scheme to burden you with guilt and shame as regards your secret life with God. He tries to tell you that you're a failure or a hypocrite when, in reality, you're walking the same pilgrimage that the greatest saints of history have traversed before you. To put it bluntly, sometimes prayer is boring and Bible reading is like eating sawdust.

But here's the good part: *One day of exhilaration in the Holy Spirit is worth a thousand days of struggle!* "For a day in Your courts is better than a thousand" (Psalm 84:10). It's really true.

Once God touches you with His Spirit and energizes you with His word, you're hopelessly hooked. You don't care how long this desert might last, you're going to keep walking because you know on the other side is an oasis of heavenly delights.

Now here's even better news: *The more you persevere in the secret place, the very nature of your relationship with the Lord begins to change—and the bad days get fewer and further inbetween!* There's a threshold to cross in which, once you cross it, the thrill of the secret place grabs your spirit and you gain unparalleled momentum in connecting with God.

The point is, if you stay with it, eventually you'll "hit pay dirt." Eventually the breakthrough will come. There may be a lot of boring hours between here and there, but don't quit. The greatest things in life—those things that carry eternal value—always come at the steepest price.

Boredom? Small price to pay!

27

The Secret of Feeling Attractive to God

When you come before God, how does He look at you? Your answer to that question is vitally important to the success of your secret life with God, and the accuser knows it. The accuser wants you to see a Father who is harsh, demanding, never satisfied with your performance, mostly disappointed with you, and frustrated with the rate of your spiritual growth.

If that caricature of your heavenly Father is even close to the image you carry on the inside, that false idea of how God views you will begin to drive your emotional responses to Him. You will be wearied with trying to please Him, and your spirit will not soar in the liberty of loving adoration that He has designed for you.

Nothing is deadlier to the secret place than a false idea of how God views you; and nothing is more powerfully energizing than when your mind is renewed in the word of God and you come to understand how He looks on you. *When you gain ownership of the fact that God is smiling on you, that He is desiring your company, and that He longs to be intimate with you, then the truth of that reality starts to touch your emotional chemistry, and you actually begin to feel attractive to God!* This attainment has the power to change everything about how you relate to God.

It all starts with understanding how God feels about the cross of Christ. Revelation 5:6 describes Jesus as a Lamb standing before the eternal throne "as though it had been slain." In other words, the death of Christ is as fresh to God's mind as the day it happened. Time will never erase from before God's eyes the immediacy of the horror of Calvary, and the powerful atoning work of the blood of Christ. God is eternally and infinitely passionate about His Son's cross! Those who place their faith in this great demonstration of love come under the intense favor of God Almighty. Your faith in Christ's sacrifice unlocks the infinite passions and delights of an exuberant God who yearns to be joined to your heart in eternal affection. Because you have set your love upon the One whom the Father has set His love upon, you now have an automatic "in" with God. You're His child; you're family.

When you know you're attractive to God, you come into His presence with boldness. You come into His presence the way He wants you to, with a lifted face, with expectant eyes, with a delighted smile, with an eager voice, and with a burning heart.

He doesn't enjoy you any less because you struggle. He knows your weakness, He sees your failures, but yet He owns you as His child and enjoys you even when you fall! He loves it when you pick yourself up and keep stepping forward again into His arms. How comforting to know we can bring the entire package of our inadequacies and shortcomings into His presence and know that He lovingly embraces us and delights in us! He enjoys us at every stage of the maturity process.

Psalm 45:11 tells us how our beloved Lord feels when He looks at us: "So the King will greatly desire your beauty." This is how the King looks at His bride who has left everything in order to be joined to her Husband. *You are stunningly beautiful to Jesus!* When He looks upon your beauty, He longs to have you and hold you, for ever and ever. When you come to the secret place, you are coming into the chambers of the King who finds you both beautiful and desirable. Not only do you long for His presence, He longs for yours!

Maybe we could call this "the secret of appeal." It's the secret of understanding that He finds us appealing. This understanding empowers us to desire His chambers on a continual basis. As we come into His glorious presence we are changed into His image (2 Corinthians 3:18), and the continual transformation into Christ's image causes us to be—if it were possible—even *more* attractive to Him! As the bride adorns herself with "the beauties of holiness" (Psalm 110:3), the lavish affections of a lovesick God are only intensified. *What 1 Peter 3:3 calls "the hidden person of the heart" is made increasingly beautiful in the hidden place of the Most High, where "the incorruptible beauty of a gentle and quiet spirit" is perfected through intimacy.*

It's here that the bride begins to cry, "Set me as a seal upon your heart" (Song of Solomon 8:6). The bride is saying to her Beloved, "Cause Your life to be bound up in my life. Cause the primary affections of Your heart to be fastened upon me. Make me the center of Your universe. I don't want You to feel anything without including me. I want to share every passion of Your heart. I want Your thoughts to become my thoughts. I want to be joined to You in love."

It's a cry to become His soul mate. A soul mate is someone who not only arrives at the same conclusions as you, but who gets to those conclusions the same way you do. They think like you. Their line of reasoning aligns with yours. You have the same thought processes and responses to life situations. Jesus is turning His bride into His soul mate, and the secret place is where that love is incubated and enflamed.

Not only are you attractive to Jesus, but you are also embraced passionately by your heavenly Father! He describes you as "the apple of His eye" (Deuteronomy 32:10; Zechariah 2:8), which means He guards and values you as you do the very pupil of your eye.

The description of Jacob's preoccupation with his son Benjamin parallels our Father's preoccupation with us:

> "Now therefore, when I come to your servant my father, and the lad is not with us, since his life is bound up in the lad's

life, it will happen, when he sees that the lad is not with us, that he will die. So your servants will bring down the gray hair of your servant our father with sorrow to the grave" (Genesis 44:30-31).

They said of Jacob that "his life is bound up in the lad's life." Jacob represents your heavenly Father. Your Father's life is also "bound up" in the life of His beloved children. He lives when He sees that you live; He thrills when He sees you fulfilled; He rejoices when you are liberated; He is content when you are at rest. He construed this awesome thing called "redemption" because His heart is bound up in yours. You are the center of God's universe!

Jesus testified to this truth when He prayed to the Father, "'That the world may know that You…have loved them as You have loved Me'" (John 17:23). Think of it! God loves us just as much as He loves His only begotten Son! He feels the same way about us that He feels about His holy, spotless, selfless Son. Incredible!!

God feels much more deeply and passionately about me than I do about Him. Even when my passions are burning hot and bright for Him, they do not approach the intensity of His love for me. Here's one way I've noticed this to be true. The intensity of my love is very limited because I can only think upon one thing at a time. So when I work or go about the duties of the day, cognitive thoughts of God actually disappear totally from my mind. My mind will return to the Lord a few hours later, but for certain periods of time I'm not even thinking about Him. *But He never stops thinking about me.* His eyes are constantly riveted on me, and His mind is incessantly focused on who I am and who He is making me to be. When I return to thoughts of Him, the immediate witness of the Spirit is, "I've been here all along, waiting for you. I love you so much!"

He waits for you to come to Him! He waits all night long, watching over you, waiting for you to rise, hoping that He might be the first thought of your morning. You don't have to wonder if He wants you to come into the secret place. He has been waiting for you, and He'll continue to wait for as long as necessary—because His heart is bound up in your life.

May you have grace from above to truly own the reality of this powerful secret: God finds you attractive! "Lord, may I never again withhold myself from Your embrace!"

Part III

Setting A Marathon Pace

Secrets of the Secret Place

In Section II, we considered some very practical tips for making the most of the secret place. Now, let's ask ourselves how we can prepare our hearts to make a lifetime commitment to the secret place. We don't want merely a burst of fresh energy, only to have it dissipate in a few weeks. We want the resolve of pursuing God in the secret place every single day of our lives until we're called home.

28

The Secret of Desperation

For many years I was very disciplined in my devotional life, determined to spend time daily in the word and prayer. I would read through the entire Bible in a different translation every year. I would worship the Lord in song and would pray through a long list of people. However, I never discovered the highest joys of the secret place until the Lord took me on an unplanned journey. He allowed a calamity to hit my life that traumatized me. My life careened out of control, and my very survival (spiritually) was at stake. Frantically, I began to claw and push my way into God's heart, scouring the Bible cover to cover to understand His ways. It felt like I was fighting for air like a drowning man. To put it simply, I had been made desperate. It was in this desperate pursuit of God that the secret place began to blossom for me like a desert flower. What made the difference in my own journey? In one word, it was *desperation*.

Desperation will turn you into a different person. A drowning man has only one thought on his mind—how to get air. Nothing else matters to him. Life's priorities become very simple. The hemmoraging woman of Mark 5:25 was willing to press her way through the crowd because the only thing that mattered was touching Jesus. Desperation produces tunnel vision. When God

chased away the Syrian army from the city of Samaria, the Israelites in Samaria had become so desperate from hunger during the
siege that they trampled to death the officer at the gate in their
rush for food (see 2 Kings 6-7).

When you are made desperate for God, your pursuit of God
takes on a different quality. When it's personal survival that's at
stake, you begin to seek Jesus in a different way. You get a look in
your eye that appears half-crazed to others. You're willing to go
anywhere or do anything. No pricetag is too high. You look at
other people and think, "I love you, I respect you, I think you're a
very nice person—but if you don't get out of my way I'm going to
run you over. Because I have *got* to touch Jesus!"

Banal sources of entertainment, such as television and mov-
ies, have to go. Invitations to parties are spurned. Others start to
pull away because you're not as much fun as you used to be. But
it's irrelevant to you because you're desperate for God. Nothing
else matters right now except touching the hem of Jesus' garment. Desperate people don't struggle with the same distractions
and hindrances as the general population. A desperate person
would never say, "I struggle to find time for the secret place." Or,
"I get easily distracted by everyday demands." Such petty distractions could never hinder someone who is desperate. The normal
hindrances of life don't even faze a desperate one because of the
single-focused intensity of the pursuit.

When you begin to seek God with this kind of desperation,
powerful spiritual winds begin to blow around your life. You're
setting off a storm! Things begin to change inside you at an unprecedented rate. Angelic activity (both good and evil) surrounding your life becomes intense, even though you may not be aware
of it. You gain the attention of heaven and hell. Issues that sim-
mered on low for many years suddenly come to a head, screaming for resolve. You find yourself surrounded by suspicion and
reproach. God has you in His accelerated class, and the speed of
change and transition surrounding your life is dizzying.

And what's happening on the inside? You're coming alive to
the word of God! His word is feeding and sustaining you. New
insights are electrifying and carrying you. The closeness of His

presence begins to intoxicate you. The revelation of His love for you is redefining your relationship with Him. The understanding of His heart and purposes is giving you a whole new perspective on the kingdom of God. You're becoming addicted to the glories of the secret place!

Someone reading these words is thinking right now, "Lord, how do I touch what Bob is talking about right here?" I can only speak from personal experience. There was nothing I could do to touch this desperation. I needed God's intervention. I needed Him to make me desperate. I called on Him, and He answered me. It all begins and ends in the heart of God. "For it is God who works in you both to will and to do for His good pleasure" (Philippians 2:13).

I'm inviting you to pray a crazy prayer—a dangerous prayer. "Lord, make me desperate for You!" If you will cry out to Him from the depths of your heart, He will hear you. He knows exactly where you're at, He knows how much you can bear, and He is able to craft an answer to that prayer that will produce a great cry of desperation within your soul. He knows how to make us hungry!

You need not fear the consequences of this prayer of holy consecration. "Perfect love casts out fear." Perfect love knows that anything coming from God's hand is for our good and benefit, so perfect love fears nothing that God would give in order to extract a greater devotion and consecration from us. Let Him perfect you in His love so that you might throw wide your arms and embrace His good, acceptable, and perfect will.

When we enter a season of distress, our first response is to cry out for relief. However, God does not always bring immediate relief because He destines the distress to produce desperation within us. This truth reminds me of a recent dialogue with a friend, Cindy Nelson. Cindy suffered in her body for many years but then was sovereignly healed. She is intensely grateful to God for her healing, and now ministers to people who live with chronic pain. However, her observations about her secret life with God since her healing were very intriguing to me. She has given me permission to reproduce her email exactly as she wrote it to me:

"Just recently I realized that I lost the desperation that I used to seek God with before God healed me. I remember depending on every word, every breath from God to sustain me. I stormed the gates of heaven to hear from Him. To hear hope, strength, peace, something that would assure me of His presence and keep me going. My need was so great and I realized that He alone could meet my needs. I still know this but I have become less dependent upon Him. I recently had to repent. I don't necessarily want another tragedy in my life to draw me back to that desperation, (I certainly know better.) But I know difficult times reveal one's dependence on God. In some respects I think my quiet times with God were richer than compared to now. It is different. Less intense is really the only way I can describe it."

I have read the stories of believers who were imprisoned for many years for their faith who, after their release, wept over the loss of the intimacy with God that they once had while in prison. The Lord was so close to them in prison, and now in their freedom everything was different. They missed the former intimacy so much that some of them longed to return to prison! *While none of us asks God for hardship, we can't deny the fact that hardship produces desperation, which in turn produces intense intimacy.*

I am not saying hardship is the only pathway to desperation. God has many ways to answer our prayers. But I am saying that one of the greatest secrets to unlocking the inner life with God is through desperation. The wise will seek Him with desperate longing. Here is to be found the path of life.

29

The Secret of Manna Gathering

When you're desperate for God, you become dependent upon the daily sustaining power of His word. Your source of survival is your daily manna—feeding on the word of God. We know the manna of the wilderness was good for only one day; if kept over into the next day, it would rot (Exodus 16:12-31). It's still true that yesterday's feeding in the word will never sustain us for today. One of the primary functions of the secret place is to be fed afresh each day in His word.

Proverbs 16:26 says, "The person who labors, labors for himself, for his hungry mouth drives him on." It's our hunger for the word that drives us into the secret place. When we are hungry spiritually, we are energized to labor in the word. A lack of hunger is a danger sign. When someone is sick, often the first symptom of their sickness is a loss of hunger. Those who lose their spiritual hunger need a medical exam, spiritually speaking. Is a cancerous sin destroying their spiritual vitality? What is true in the natural is also true in the spiritual. By drinking lots of water (the Holy Spirit), getting plenty of rest (ceasing from our own works), exercising ourselves in the word, avoiding junk foods (lousy replacements), often our spiritual appetite can be restored. *Spiritual hunger is absolutely essential to spiritual health be-*

cause without it we won't be motivated to feed on the manna of God's word.

It's vitally important that each one of us learn how to collect manna for himself. Those who view the Sunday morning sermon as their source of nutrition are certain to be spiritual skeletons. *God never intended that we live off the secret life of our pastor; He wants us to uncover the lifegiving thrill of feeding ourselves daily in His word.*

Once you learn to feed yourself in the word, you are no longer upset when the Sunday sermon doesn't apply to your life. You weren't looking for the sermon to be your source of feeding and life anyways. If something in the sermon feeds you, you reckon it a bonus. You're no longer dependent on others to give you milk because now you are cutting off your own meat.

Many Americans have misplaced expectations of what Sunday morning church is all about. They're looking for a place to be taught in the word, to be filled up, and a place for their kids to be taught and strengthened. But often they are expecting out of Sunday morning church what God intended for them to get in the secret place and at the family altar. (By "family altar" I am referring to parents sitting down daily with their children to instruct them in the word and pray together, according to the commandment of Scripture.) When we place higher expectations upon Sunday morning church than it can sustain, we can easily become critical or even cynical toward the body of Christ (a disease which can be terminal and is highly infectious, especially with our children).

It's not that difficult to learn how to gather manna. Just get out there and start working. Pick up your Bible, and begin to labor in it. At first you will feel clumsy, but keep persevering. *The more you labor in the word, the more adept you'll become at gathering the daily portion that will satisfy your soul.* You learn to gather by getting out in the field and just doing it.

As you persevere, you will discover that the Lord designed the secret place to satisfy your heart in at least three ways:

Feeding In The Word

Of the godly it is said, "But his delight is in the law of the LORD, and in His law he meditates day and night. He shall be like a tree planted by the rivers of water, that brings forth its fruit in its season, whose leaf also shall not wither; and whatever he does shall prosper" (Psalm 1:2-3). As we meditate and feed in the word of God, we are like trees that produce fruit because we have nutrients flowing into us.

Drinking In The Spirit

Jesus said, "'But whoever drinks of the water that I shall give him will never thirst. But the water that I shall give him will become in him a fountain of water springing up into everlasting life'" (John 4:14). *The Holy Spirit is like the water that helps us swallow the manna of the word.* Feeding in the word must always be complemented with drinking of the Spirit.

Cultivating A Knowing Relationship With God

Hebrews 8:11 quotes the Old Testament, "'None of them shall teach his neighbor, and none his brother, saying, "Know the LORD," for all shall know Me, from the least of them to the greatest of them.'" God wants to lead you into a hidden place in Him where you develop your own unique connection with Him, and you come to know Him totally independently of everyone else. He wants you to develop your own secret history of communing with Him and knowing Him. No man is to teach you how to find this knowing relationship with God; the Holy Spirit Himself will be your teacher. All you must do is shut your door.

Oh, the awesome depths of communion that we can find in the secret place—not to mention the ingesting of delightsome spirit food! When we properly find these things in the secret place and lead our families in these things, then Sunday morning gatherings can fulfill their proper role in our lives: a place where God is glorified and ministered to, a place where we can encourage and support others, a place where the vision for our collective body is articulated, a place where our unity is built, a place of corporate prayer, a place where the young and weak are strengthened and encouraged, and a place where seekers can come to Christ.

Just one more quick thought. I remember the days when I, as a pastor, would glean the word daily for potential sermon material. I was always looking for truths that would feed my congregation. But then the Lord arrested me and changed how I come to the word. Now, I read the Bible just for me. I'm so hungry for Him that every day I must be sustained by fresh manna from the word. If I don't get my manna for the day, I get a little bit on the cranky side. So now I gather manna just for me. But here's what I've found: When I share with others the manna that has nurtured me, it feeds them as well! In fact, I've discovered that others appear much more fed when I share with them that which first sustained me. *The secret is: Learn to gather your own manna. Then you'll have something to share.*

30

The Secret of Enduring

A s we poise ourselves for the full marathon of the Christian race, not only must we gather our daily manna, we must also grow in the Christlike quality of *endurance*.

We all have desert seasons in God when everything in our spiritual life is dry, dusty, and void of inspiration. The only way through is to make a decision in advance that no matter how tough the slogging gets, we're never going to give up on our pursuit of God. We're going to abide in Christ no matter what. I'll let you in on a secret: This kind of tenacious commitment to endurance will open the path to the most meaningful dimensions of relationship with the Lord.

Seasons not only break the monotony of sameness, they are necessary to productivity. Nothing can live in unbroken sunshine. Constant joy and happiness, with no clouds on the horizon, produces drought. Night is as important as day; the sun must be followed by clouds and rain. Nonstop sunshine only creates a desert. We don't enjoy storms, but they're an essential part of a complete life, and the key to victory comes in finding how to weather the storms of life in such a way that they don't dislodge us from our secret life in God.

It's easy to endure in the good times. It's when the hard times hit that our endurance is proven. When times get tough, it's tempting to neglect the secret place. Jesus, however, manifested precisely the opposite tendency. When He was hurting, He sought out the place of prayer. His time in Gethsemane is a great example of this, of which it was recorded, "And being in agony, He prayed more earnestly" (Luke 22:44). When Jesus was hurting, He prayed. When He hurt real hard, He prayed even harder. *This was Jesus' secret to enduring the horror of His sufferings. He prepared Himself through prayer to endure the pain.* If we respond properly, distress can actually be a gift. Pain can provide tremendous impetus to pray—if we will allow it to catapult us into God's face instead of polarizing us away from Him.

Paul prayed the Colossian believers would be "strengthened with all might, according to His glorious power, for all patience and longsuffering with joy" (Colossians 1:11). One of the greatest challenges, in the place of hardship, is to suffer a long time *with joy*. It's not possible in human strength! Which is why Paul prayed that they might be "strengthened with all might," for it takes the might of God to rejoice through long durations of painful hardship. Being joyful in suffering is a godly quality, for God Himself is "patience and longsuffering with joy." Consider how much God suffers as He shares the grief of the world and for how long He has thus suffered! And yet although His suffering is stronger than any of us realize, He is also filled with great joy. Only God can suffer so much with such joy.

When we are called to endure with joy, it is imperative we find the solace of the secret place. Here it is that we are filled and "strengthened with all might" that we might suffer long. Simply put, godly endurance is impossible apart from a well-nurtured secret life with God.

Hardship can be embraced with joy, in my opinion, only when we understand God's purpose in the pain. "My brethren, count it all joy when you fall into various trials, *knowing* that the testing of your faith produces patience" (James 1:2-3). The only way to be joyful in trials is through "knowing"—knowing God's purpose in it. How do we learn God's purposes in our sufferings? The secret pursuit of God in His word is what will reveal purpose to us. As we see how He carried Bible saints along through their hardships, we begin to see His heart for carrying us through to the same kinds of glorious victories. The thing that enabled Paul to endure his "thorn in the flesh" was God unfolding His purpose to Paul for the thorn. Once Paul saw purpose, he could cooperate with God's grace.

Paul coined a fascinating term, "the patience...of the Scriptures." It's found in Romans 15:4, "For whatever things were written before were written for our learning, that we through the patience and comfort of the Scriptures might have hope." The original word for "patience" (Greek, *hupomone*) means, "constancy, perseverance, continuance, bearing up, steadfastness, patient endurance." The Scriptures are my source of constancy. Every time I return to them, I am renewed in my posture of waiting on God alone. Not only do the Scriptures bear me up and enable me to endure, but the witness of of God's purposes and ways is consistent from Genesis to Revelation. When I see the unbroken pattern of Scripture, that God eventually reveals His salvation to those who endure, I am strengthened in hope. The Scriptures speak of the patience of the saints so frequently that the Scriptures themselves are said to be patient!

The Bible commends those who seek to understand the path God has set for them. "The wisdom of the prudent is to understand his way" (Proverbs 14:8). It is in the sanctuary of His presence that we gain understanding into life's enigmas (Psalm 73:17). *The sanctuary of His embrace is where God reveals purpose, which in turn empowers us to endure hardship with joy for we know He is working it all together for good* (Romans 8:28).

One of the scriptural symbols for this process is *pearl*. Pearl is formed within an oyster which has experienced the distress of a foreign particle of sand getting stuck within its shell. Pearl represents the eternally valuable change God works within us in the place of hardship. There is nothing else that changes us quite so readily and profoundly as a devotion to the secret place in the midst of grueling hardship.

The longer the irritant resides within the oyster's shell, the more valuable the pearl becomes. *Therefore, the formative value of tribulation is sometimes directly proportional to the duration of the crucible.* The longer the distress, the more valuable the pearl. It is the confidence of this reality which empowers us to persevere with joy. When we endure in love through hardship, we qualify to enter the gates of pearl—for the only way to enter the eternal city is through the pearly gates of "treasure perfected in hardship."

The apostle John provides a gripping example of the reward of enduring in the secret place, even in the face of hardship. In his old age, John was exiled to "the island that is called Patmos for the word of God and for the testimony of Jesus Christ" (Revelation 1:9). There can be no question that he struggled in his 90-year-old frame with the rigors of an island prison. He suffered in his body, felt the pangs of loneliness, and inevitably felt like he was ending out his days in pointless futility. Merely existing on this island was not his idea of a strong finish in the race. However, instead of succumbing to self-preoccupation or discouragement, he "was in the Spirit on the Lord's Day" (Revelation 1:10). In other words, he was proactively enduring the hardship by devoting himself to his secret place love relationship with his Beloved.

What was God's response to John's endurance and patience? God honored him by granting him an unparalleled revelation of the beauty and glory of Christ Jesus (I am referring to the Book of Revelation). It was as though God was saying, "I honor those who give their love to Me in the secret place while persevering in the fire of hardship and suffering. I reward them by empowering them to behold the light of the knowledge of the glory of My majesty that is found in the face of My wonderful Son."

Don't ever give up! Today may be the day when He rewards your devotion with a sublime revelation of the eternal glory of the Man, Christ Jesus our Lord! Through the might of God's Spirit, *any* hardship can be endured with joy for the extravagance of such a reward.

31

The Secret of Confinement

L ike John on the isle of Patmos, some saints are finding themselves in places of restriction in this hour, and are struggling with all the emotional trappings that attend imprisonment and confinement. Feelings such as hopelessness, uselessness, despair, abandonment, rejection, reproach, lack of understanding, loneliness, vulnerability, etc. With such a host of emotions assaulting the prisoner's equilibrium, it's difficult to maintain an unswerving confidence in the simple secret of this chapter: *When you're in confinement, God is closer to you than you realize.*

The Lord assures the afflicted soul, "'I will be with him in trouble'" (Psalm 91:15). When you've been troubled by circumstances that twist and press your soul, be assured that your Lord is closer to you than ever!

David said of the Lord, "He made darkness His secret place" (Psalm 18:11). When the lights of understanding go out and you're plunged into emotional darkness, you are actually being issued an invitation into God's secret place. It's in the darkness where God meets in secret with His chosen ones.

The Lord's prison is generally characterized by social isolation and loneliness. Friends drift away, and relationships that once ministered life and grace to you are distant or estranged. Your ability to function is greatly curtailed, and you find no joy in the small amount of movement that your chains grant you. This confinement, however, has been orchestrated by your Lover. Your heavenly Husband will allure you into the wilderness (as per Hosea 2), He will comfort you with His presence, and He will renew your affections for His goodness and glory. It is here, in the pain of loneliness and aimlessness, that the Lord designs to ignite a depth of love relationship like you've never known. Before, you were too busy to find it or care about it. Now, you're so determined to understand the nature of His hand in your life that you're pressing into Him with abandonment and desperation.

In His kindness, He dries up every other fountain that has nurtured your soul, that He might become your only fountain in the quietness of this cell. It's here you will learn to own the reality of Psalm 87:7, "All my springs are in You." Instead of being energized by projects, you will now become energized by a Person. Being with Him and in Him will become your criteria for success.

David spoke of the intimacy of the prison: "You have hedged me behind and before, and laid Your hand upon me. Such knowledge is too wonderful for me; it is high, I cannot attain it" (Psalm 139:5-6). Being hedged behind, David cannot stop or quit because he is being herded forward. Being hedged before, he cannot accelerate or push ahead, he can only move forward at the pace the Lord sovereignly sets for him. He can't work up momentum, and he can't quit. Then, he's under the mighty hand of God, which means he can't move to the left or right either. He is a man without options. And his evaluation of this place of constraint, restraint, and harnessed direction? David could have been tempted to view this as highly constrictive and controlling, but instead he called it such high knowledge that he cannot attain it! The Shulamite described it in this way, "His left hand is under my head, and his right hand embraces me" (Song of Solomon 8:3). She viewed the restrictions as the loving embrace of His arms. *Instead of focusing on the immobility, the prisoner is fo-*

cusing on the glorious intimacy of being held so firmly in the Lord's hands. The confinement is actually a gift!

Not only is this prison a place of intense intimacy, *but it is also a place of revelational impartation.* Jesus said, "'Whatever I tell you in the dark, speak in the light'" (Matthew 10:27). In the place of darkness, God is saying more to you than you realize! While He might not be talking about what you *want* Him to talk about, He is desiring to download to you the thoughts and intents of *His* heart. If you listen and hear in the darkness, one day you will speak in the light what He whispered to your heart in the dark.

Are you in a prison of sorts? Just give Him your love! The Scripture says, "A friend loves at all times" (Proverbs 17:17). Even when the Lord is mysterious in His ways, His friends still love Him. And in the quietness of that love, a new depth of intimacy is cultivated and established in the heart that will carry you for life. You will learn that "Faithful are the wounds of a friend" (Proverbs 27:6), for He loved you enough to wound you, that He might woo you into a greater connection with Him.

Here's one of the secrets of darkness: *He imprisons those He loves in order to awaken them in the secret place to mature bridal affections.* Don't despise your chains, for they bind you to the heart of the One you long for. You are the prisoner of the Lord.

The Secret of Waiting

The secret place is a time machine, transporting us from our time zone to His. Here we step into the eternal and begin to view all of life from the perspective of the Ageless One who is without beginning or ending of days. From this vantage, waiting on God takes on an entirely different hue.

The closer you get to God, the more you realize He's in no hurry. *There is no frenetic hurrying in heaven, only calculated purpose.* "Whoever believes will not act hastily" (Isaiah 28:16). Those who step into God's time zone will not allow urgent matters to press them into acting too quickly and getting ahead of God.

Lord, help me to write about the powerful secret of waiting on You!

Many of us approach our secret place with a checklist of activities, and we "check them off" mentally once they're completed:

> Confession of sins
> Worship, praise, thanksgiving
> Bible Reading
> Meditation
> Intercession
> Journaling

Then, once we've completed everything on our list, our time in the secret place is finished. But is it *really* finished? There is yet another element to be included—waiting on God.

One of the best descriptions of waiting on God is found in Psalm 123:2, "Behold, as the eyes of servants look to the hand of their masters, as the eyes of a maid to the hand of her mistress, so our eyes look to the LORD our God, until He has mercy on us." *To wait on God is to stare at His hand.* We stare at His hand for two primary reasons: to serve and minister to Him in whatever way His hand might signal us to fulfill; and to wait until He moves His mighty hand on our behalf. Waiting on God is not watching television until God chooses to move; waiting on God is attentively gazing upon Him with undistracted focus until He has mercy on us. And until He acts, we just wait on Him and love Him. I would say it this way: While waiting *for* God, wait *on* God.

Someone once said, "We should seek His face and not His hand." I disagree. We seek His face *and* His hand. We seek the intimacy of His face, but we also seek the power of His hand. It's not either/or; it's both/and. We so long for the release of His power that we gaze with rapt attention upon Him until He moves on our behalf.

Waiting on God may be the most difficult of all the spiritual disciplines, and perhaps that's the reason so few truly practice it. Just sitting in His presence and gazing…it can be agonizing to us who have become accustomed to being bombarded with data and stimuli. We lack the attention span to wait on God. But He knows that, so in His kindness He designs scenarios that will help us learn how to wait on Him. *Once we press through and cross the boredom threshold, we open to the joys and adventures of waiting on God.*

To wait on God successfully, we must come to derive more fulfillment by being with Him than by working for Him. When being with Him fully satisfies us, we can wait for as long as necessary—just as long as He stays with us. This is why Jesus could wait to minister until He was thirty. He was totally satisfied in His relationship with His Father, so He was willing to wait even though He was ready to minister long before age thirty. I think

Jesus could have just as easily waited until He was ninety to begin His ministry because the presence and affection of His Father made Him complete.

Some of the greatest assurances of Scripture are offered to those who wait on God.

> For since the beginning of the world men have not heard nor perceived by the ear, nor has the eye seen any God besides You, who acts for the one who waits for Him (Isaiah 64:4).

> Therefore the LORD will wait, that He may be gracious to you; and therefore He will be exalted, that He may have mercy on you. For the LORD is a God of justice; blessed are all those who wait for Him (Isaiah 30:18).

Regarding the latter verse, I have heard some teach, "You're waiting for God, but God's waiting for you!" While that may be true in some instances, it is not the truth of Isaiah 30:18. When it says, "The Lord will wait," it doesn't mean that God is waiting for you to do something; it means that God is strategically delaying His miraculous visitation because He has greater things in store for you than you've even asked for. But to give you the fullness of what He has planned for your life, He will use the season of waiting to prepare you as a vessel, and also to prepare circumstances around your life so that you will be able to step forward into the proper sphere when His release comes to you. He's waiting so that He can crown you with an even greater blessing.

Many today commonly embrace the idiom, "It is insanity to keep doing what you've always done and expect different results." While that statement may be true in some arenas, it is not true when it comes to waiting on God. Waiting on God is so powerful that the enemy will do everything in His power to dissuade you from maintaining your watch. He will tell you that you're insane to keep waiting on God in the midst of your pressing circumstances. He'll tell you that waiting on God is changing nothing. But those who know the ways of God are aware of Joseph's testimony: Even though you may wait on God for many years, there is a day coming when God will change everything in a moment of time! He may take seemingly forever to get around to it, but once God moves, He can change everything in a day.

One of the greatest incentives of waiting on God is found in Psalm 104:4, "Who makes...His ministers a flame of fire." The original word for "ministers" (Hebrew, *sharat*) speaks of someone who waits on, who serves, ministers, attends. So *sharat* hints of intimacy, referring to those servants who serve in closest proximity to the king. *And here's what God does with His ministers who wait on Him: He makes them a flame of fire! He ignites them with the passions of His heart and enflames them with zeal for His face and for His kingdom.*

God's flaming zeal empowers us to wait on Him. Some of God's most powerful angels, who burn with zeal for Him, are described in the book of Revelation as standing at their post—where they've been standing and waiting for centuries—until the time when God signals their release (Revelation 8:2; 19:17). They are enflamed with zeal *so they can wait.* God is setting you ablaze with His fiery passions in this hour in order that you might wait upon Him in holy passion and fiery ecstacy.

Take to heart the counsel of King David who, after years of proving this truth in his own life, left a legacy of wisdom for all men and women to follow. Receive it from a man who knew: "Wait on the LORD; be of good courage, and He shall strengthen your heart; wait, I say, on the LORD!" (Psalm 27:14).

The Secret of Tears

One of the greatest gifts you can bring to your King is the gift of absolute sincerity. I'm talking about a purity of heart that says, "Lord, I'm coming to You because You really *are* the center of my universe. You truly are all that I live for. My heart is totally and fully set upon You." Nothing surpasses the delight of being able to sing songs of total consecration with absolute abandon.

Feelings of sincerity are quickly defused when we allow the flesh to defile our conscience. No earthly pleasure is worth a defiled conscience. Feelings of guilt arise when we feel hypocritical before God—when we've spurned His overtures in order to gratify the desires of the flesh. Oh what delight when we can come boldly before His throne with a clean conscience! Even though we're not yet perfected and even though we struggle with weakness, our hearts reach for Him with impassioned desire.

I call this "sweet sincerity." This sincerity of heart has settled the issue once and for all: Jesus truly is the great love of my heart. This sincerity is "sweet" because when you know you're totally sincere in coming to God, you feel the sweetness of His reciprocating love. This is when "love [is] without hypocrisy" (Romans 12:9). I have personally found my awareness of His presence to

132

be strongest when I have had great yearning of heart for Him. *When my soul longs for Him in sweet sincerity, even to tears, my awareness of His reciprocating affections is heightened.*

True love must function in total sincerity, void of duplicity or adulterous passions. This is why we must find those measures that evoke our sense of sweet sincerity before the Lord. Now, here's the beauty of it: *When love is without hypocrisy, the sweetness of this sincerity is often accompanied by tears.*

Of the seven psalms that refer to tears, three are attributed to David's pen. The man who had an absolutely sincere secret life with God was a man of tears. David cried, "Do not be silent at my tears" (Psalm 39:12), as though his tears commended his sincerity to God. Clearly tears are not for women only. Another psalmist expressed the sincerity of his cry by pointing to his tears: "My tears have been my food day and night, while they continually say to me, 'Where is your God?'" (Psalm 42:3).

There's something about tears that is pure and unfeigned. I suppose it's possible, in a technical sense, to fake tears (as actors learn to do), but let's be honest about it: Nobody is about to fake tears while praying. When it comes to the secret place, tears are either honest or they're absent.

So the presence of tears is a profound statement to your departed Bridegroom. *Tears are liquid words.* Tears say more than words often can. Whereas words can sometimes contain the pretense of plastic platitudes, tears come straight from the heart.

Have you known tears? You are blessed. Do you struggle to find tears? Then ask for them. It's a request He will graciously fulfill.

We cry because we desire or because we're in pain; so tears are the language of desire. We desire Him, even to tears. If we lack that desire, He will cultivate it within us by seemingly withdrawing from us in His mercy. *It's famine that makes us hungry; it's drought that makes us thirsty. Deprivation produces desire.*

Do not despise the pain that gave you tears. Pour out your heart to Him; God is a refuge for us! Those who "love much" still wash the Lord's feet with their tears (see Luke 7:36-48).

Weeping and tears have always gained the Lord's attention. David understood this when he wrote, "Put my tears into Your bottle" (Psalm 56:8). Not only does the Lord notice our tears, He actually bottles and stores them as an everlasting witness in His presence.

There are two kinds of sickness in the Bible that produce tears. The first is mentioned in Proverbs 13:12, "Hope deferred makes the heart sick." When the hope of God's deliverance is deferred, the heart grows sick. This heartsickness produces a groaning from the depths of the spirit and is expressed in tears. These are the tears of the brokenhearted, and they are not despised by God. Heartsickness cries, "Oh God, visit me! Come to me in Your power and fulfill your word in my life!"

The other sickness that produces tears is seen in Song Of Solomon 5:8, "I charge you, O daughters of Jerusalem, if you find my beloved, that you tell him I am lovesick!" Lovesickness is the consequence of our Lord's restrained self-revelation, who reveals Himself to us dimly as through a veil or a dark glass. When the heart is awakened to the beauty of the King and the eyes long to behold Him, but He reveals Himself in but a fraction of His fullness, the saint becomes sick with love. Lovesickness cries, "Show me Your glory, Lord! I want to see You, I want to know You!"

Heartsickness is the product of unrequited power; lovesickness is the consequence of unrequited love. David articulated both passions when, during his years of hiding in the wilderness, he cried, "So I have looked for You in the sanctuary, to see *Your power* and *Your glory*" (Psalm 63:2). *Heartsickness weeps, "Show me Your hand!" Lovesickness weeps, "Show me Your face!"*

I am told the story of a certain young man who was seeking a breakthrough in his life in a certain area, but had exhausted all he knew to do to gain spiritual breakthrough. He wrote General William Booth (founder of The Salvation Army) for advice. The General wrote back two simple words, "Try tears."

William Booth had learned the secret. The inner chamber of prayer gains its impetus from the liquid power of tears. Do you long for a greater reality in your walk with God? Try tears.

The Secret of Holiness

Who may ascend into the hill of the LORD? Or who may stand in His holy place? He who has clean hands and a pure heart, who has not lifted up his soul to an idol, nor sworn deceitfully (Psalm 24:3-4).

LORD, who may abide in Your tabernacle? Who may dwell in Your holy hill? He who walks uprightly, and works righteousness, and speaks the truth in his heart (Psalm 15:1-2).

Nothing compares with the quintessential privilege of standing before the throne of God. It is the greatest of all honors and the highest of all delights. Demons envy the favor you have with God, and angels gape in wonder at your status in God's presence. And it's all because you have embraced His call to holiness! You have purified your heart, cleansed your hands, sprinkled your conscience with His blood, and have made yourself ready with white robes of righteous deeds.

The Lord has said, "He who walks in a perfect way, he shall serve me" (Psalm 101:6). This is not referring to sinless perfection, but rather to a blameless lifestyle that is not subject to reproach or criticism by those who live closest to you. The reward of this consecration is the exhilarating intimacy of standing continually in His presence. This pursuit of holiness is not a burden but rather a profound privilege. *Happy holiness is one of the quiet secrets of the kingdom—a purity of heart that opens the pathway to the greatest heights of communion with God.*

Holiness is not an inherent quality we carry; it is a derived quality that we take on. Holiness has but one source, the Holy One. *Holiness has to do with proximity to the throne.* The seraphim are called "holy ones," not because of *who* they are but because of *where* they are. They are "holy ones" because they live in the immediate presence of the Holy One! I am holy only to the extent that I abide in His holy presence.

I used to define holiness more by what we *don't* do, but now I define it more by what we *do* do. Holiness is found in drawing near to the holy flame of the Trinity. There, anything unholy is burned like stubble, and all that is holy is enflamed and made hotter.

"For the LORD God is a sun" (Psalm 84:11). As my Sun, the Lord is my light, my warmth, the one around whom my life revolves, and He is the one who brings forth fruit from the garden of my life. His Spirit waters my life, His word nourishes my life, and His face is the power that causes the fruit of my garden to grow. As a planet revolves around the sun, I want my life to revolve around Christ. I want to be a planet, not a comet that swings by every 300 hundred years only to return to the darkness. And I don't want to be a Pluto, hanging out on the furthest fringe. I want to be close—blazing with the same holy fire that radiates from His face.

To understand holiness, we need to look at the first time the Spirit is called "Holy Spirit" in the Bible. From the very beginning, the third person of the Trinity was called "the Spirit of God" (Genesis 1:2). He was never revealed as Holy Spirit until a most unfortunate incident in the life of a remarkable man. David was heavily anointed of the Spirit, and as a prophetic psalmist he lived in the dimension of the Spirit. (He wrote both Psalm 24 and Psalm 15, quoted at the beginning of this chapter.) But David took a hard fall into sin. He committed adultery with his neighbor's wife and then killed his neighbor. Gripped with fear, he then launched a big coverup campaign to hide his sin. But during his season of denial, something terrible happened to him—the Spirit of God lifted off his life. He was accustomed to having songs of the Spirit flow from within, but the flow stopped. His prayer life became trite and unfulfilling. He knew something was terribly wrong. Then, along came Nathan the prophet who pointedly told David of his sin. When David repented, he acknowledged he had missed the presence of God's Spirit which had become so precious and so fulfilling to him. Yearning for a return to the former intimacy with God, David pled, "Do not cast me away from Your presence, and do not take Your *Holy* Spirit from me" (Psalm 51:11). This was the desperate cry of a man who learned from personal experience that the Spirit of God, above all else, is *holy*. He dwells only with those whose hearts are directed toward holiness. Holy men live in the presence of the Holy Spirit. Once you've known this intimacy, you realize that *nothing* is worth losing it!

Holiness is much more than simply clean living. *Holiness is a life lived before the throne of God.* The Scripture says of John the Baptist that "Herod feared John, knowing that he was a just and holy man" (Mark 6:20). John was not simply just (clean). He was much more than that; he was also holy. He was set apart to God, carrying the presence of God, a man of heaven living on earth. John lived in the presence of God—which is why Jesus called him "the burning and shining lamp" (John 5:35). Just and holy men cause kings to fear. They're not just pure; they also burn with the flame that emanates from their fiery abode around the throne.

Holiness is to prayer as fire is to gasoline. When a holy man or woman prays, explosive things happen. *We don't pursue holiness for the sake of power, we pursue holiness for the sake of love. But those who pursue holiness out of affection for Jesus become very influential in the courts of heaven.* James 5:16 links holiness and prayer: "The effective, fervent prayer of a righteous man avails much." Things change on earth when a holy man or woman, with a cultivated secret life in God, prays with passion and urgency to the Lord he or she has come to know and love.

God is so committed to bringing us into this holiness that He is willing to do "whatever it takes" to get us there. The Bible points out that the main purpose of God's chastening in our lives is primarily "that we may be partakers of His holiness" (Hebrews 12:10). If we will respond properly to His disciplines, they will inevitably lead us via the pathway of repentance to true holiness. When the chastening first comes, it feels like God is trying to kill us. But if we will persevere in love, crucifixion and burial is followed by resurrection!

I want to close this chapter with this powerful truth: *Holiness produces resurrection.* As certainly as chastening produces infirmity and brokenness, holiness produces resurrection, deliverance, and healing.

It says that the Lord Jesus was "declared to be the Son of God with power according to the Spirit of holiness, by the resurrection from the dead" (Romans 1:4). In other words, it was Christ's *holiness* that precipitated His resurrection. This truth was prophesied in David, "For You will not leave my soul in Sheol, nor will You allow Your *Holy One* to see corruption" (Psalm 16:10). That verse applies initially to David, who was chastened by God almost to the point of death, but then was resurrected because of his holiness. But this is actually the Holy Spirit speaking of Christ Jesus, who did not see corruption. Jesus' body experienced rigormortus, but it never experienced corruption because He rose before decay set in.

It was true of David and of Christ, and it's also true of you! You can't keep holiness buried forever. Even if you feel dead and buried under the weight of God's disciplining hand, devote yourself to His holy presence. Regardless of your shattered dreams and deferred hopes, live in the secret place of the Most High. It is the secret of your redemption. *As you love Him from your grave, you are setting powerful spiritual forces into motion.* Joseph was buried in prison, but because of his holiness they couldn't keep him buried forever. The longer you try to keep a holy man buried, the more force must be exerted to keep him there; and the more force that's exerted to keep him buried, the higher his resurrection will eventually be. Keep Joseph buried too long, and he'll rise to the heights of the palace.

The grave could hold the Holy One only until the beginning of the third day. Death's grip gave way, and Holiness rose to the highest place:

> Therefore God also has highly exalted Him and given Him the name which is above every name, that at the name of Jesus every knee should bow, of those in heaven, and of those on earth, and of those under the earth, and that every tongue should confess that Jesus Christ is Lord, to the glory of God the Father (Philippians 2:9-11).

Practice the holiness of His presence, O weary saint. It's inevitable—*holiness will rise again!*

35

The Secret of Buying Gold

"I counsel you to buy from Me gold refined in the fire, that you may be rich" (Revelation 3:18).

What is this gold that enriches us? It's the gold of authentically-produced godly character; it's *Christlikeness*. We all want to be conformed more and more into the likeness of Jesus, but there is no cheap way to become more Christlike. Godly character is not given to us; we buy it. We buy it without earthly money but yet at a steep price.

To de-mystify this thing, let me describe very clearly the process whereby we buy "gold refined in the fire." First comes the fire. By fire, I am talking about tribulation or affliction or distress or calamity or persecution. In the last days there is coming a great escalation of fire. You don't have to wonder or imagine whether you're in the fire. When the fire hits your life, you will know it! You will lose control, your pain levels will skyrocket, and your desperation for God will intensify. Your flesh will want to collapse and give up, but since your spirit is alive to the beauties of Christ, the fire will be used of God to drive you into the face of Christ like never before. Instead of giving up, you'll run even harder! Your primary source of sanity in the midst of the fire will be your secret place, where the Spirit will soothe your tortured soul and the word will sustain your hope and faith.

As you press into the word while in the fire, the word will begin to read your mail. It will locate you. It will draw a plumb line in your life, and you will begin to see areas of your heart and soul that have been out of alignment with God's ways and will. As you see those things, you are so desperate for God you gladly and diligently do business with Him, repenting and considering deeply how to change and adopt new patterns of thought, behavior, and motive. As you embrace the changes that God's Spirit inspires within you, you are actually becoming more like Jesus. Or to put it another way, you're buying gold in the fire.

It says we "buy" this gold because the pricetag is steep. The price is endurance. If we continue to press into God in the secret place—when our legs are crying out that they cannot take another step and when our lungs are screaming at us to relax the pace—then we will buy this gold. We will be changed into the image of Christ in the midst of the fire. We will lose things in the process, but what we gain will be so precious that we will consider all that we lost to be rubbish (Philippians 3:8).

When you're in the fire, it's important *how* you come to the word. Before the fire hit my life, I would come to the word to find good fodder to feed the flock I was pastoring; after the fire hit my life, I came to the word to be fed myself.

James 1:22-25 likens God's word to a mirror. We are using God's word properly when we come to it and allow it to mirror back to us the things we need to see and change within ourselves. The word was never intended for us to come to it for a third party. *It was written that we might look into it for ourselves, see the standards of Christ reflected back to us, and embrace Spirit-empowered change.*

The fire has a way of making you a doer of the word and not just a hearer only. You become desperate for a word from God, and then when it comes, you cling to it like it's your very life source. When the fire hits your life, your concern is not whether your neighbor is looking into the mirror of the word and then forgetting about it; your concern is primarily that *you* look into the word and not forget. But then something amazing happens. When you share with others how the word mirrored your own shortcomings and how you became a doer of the word in the midst of the fire, your witness will have a profound effect upon your hearers. They will be fed by your witness of what has fed you.

The secret place is the only way you'll survive the fire. And the secret of the thing is, God's word flowing into you will not only enable you to survive, it will empower you to overcome and buy eternal treasure. The secret place is God's ATM, the place where you gain access to the coffers of heaven. God has great understanding into this powerful little secret, which is why He is merciful enough to send the fire in answer to your prayers. If you will cry to Him from the depths of your being, He will send exactly the right kind of fire you need at this moment in your journey. This fire will press you into the mirror of His word that you might begin to buy the gold of "refined character."

Just your diligence to carefully read this book is doing something within you. You are being filled with hope and energized with fresh purpose. You are gaining renewed impetus to press into God. Your weakened knees and limp hands are gaining strength, and you're acquiring new momentum in your pursuit of God. You're getting it. You're running into the secret place!

36

The Secret of Inviting His Gaze

The LORD is in His holy temple, the LORD'S throne is in heaven; His eyes behold, His eyelids test the sons of men. The LORD tests the righteous, but the wicked and the one who loves violence His soul hates. Upon the wicked He will rain coals; fire and brimstone and a burning wind shall be the portion of their cup. For the LORD is righteous, He loves righteousness; His countenance beholds the upright (Psalm 11:4-7).

God scrutinizes mankind with focused intensity. He cares intensely for us and about us. He studies our responses and weighs our attitudes. He is vitally concerned over our welfare and is committed to judging us justly for every word and deed.

We can do nothing to avoid His gaze; however, it is possible to invite Him to an even greater attentiveness of our lives. Why would we want to do such a thing? Simply because His gaze is reflective of His favor. When, in the above passage, it says, "His countenance beholds the upright," you can replace the word "countenance" with "favor" (see Psalm 44:3). He looks with favor upon the upright. *To put it another way, if He likes you, He looks at you.*

The Lord has said to us, "'But on this one will I look: on him who is poor and of a contrite spirit, and who trembles at My word'" (Isaiah 66:2). When I read those words my heart moves within me, "That's me, Lord, I'm poor and contrite, and I tremble at Your word. Oh, that You would look upon me in this way!"

God is on a holy search. "For the eyes of the LORD run to and fro throughout the whole earth, to show Himself strong on behalf of those whose heart is loyal to Him" (2 Chronicles 16:9). God is looking for the perfect and loyal heart, and when He finds it, His eyes cease their searching, and they bore down with great fascination and excitement upon the one who loves Him so devoutly. Those who come under such intense scrutiny gain great favor from the Lord. He releases abundant portions of mercy, faith, grace, compassion, revelation, wisdom, might, and deliverance to those whose heart is loyal to Him.

Wise believers—those who have come to value the true treasures of the kingdom—will pant for this kind of attention. They'll stand and wave and cry, "Here, Lord, I'm over here! Come, Lord, and set Your gaze upon me!" Reclusing to the secret place is like painting a huge bull's eye on yourself. You're making a statement to heaven, "Lord, here I am. Have mercy upon me, and visit me. Lift up the light of Your countenance and look upon me, O Lord!"

Now here's the tricky part: with His favor comes His fire. When He looks upon you for good, it is with eyes ablaze. His fiery eyes can't but test you. God's fire is heartwarming and impassioning, but it's also calculatedly volatile and dangerously consuming. When God's fire explodes in your life, you can rest assured He is beholding you very closely. He is squinting at you, searching you with His eyelids, testing your every response. He is testing you to see if your heart will remain loyal to Him through the scrutiny. If you persevere, He designs to show Himself strong on your behalf (2 Chronicles 16:9).

The saint who is walking this thing out with God can appear rather ambivalent. At first he is crying out, "Search me, O God, and know my heart; try me, and know my anxieties" (Psalm 139:23). But then God's fire hits—whoooooooossh! Quickly the saint changes his tune, and his prayer sounds more like that of Job:

> "What is man, that You should exalt him, that You should set Your heart on him, that You should visit him every morning, and test him every moment? How long? Will You not look away from me, and let me alone till I swallow my saliva? Have I sinned? What have I done to You, O watcher of men? Why have You set me as Your target, so that I am a burden to myself?" (Job 7:17-20).

We desire His gaze, but then when we get it, we don't want it anymore! "Will You not look away from me, and let me alone till I swallow my saliva?" The Lord is patient with us, however, and He gives us time to process and adjust. Over time, the saint slowly begins to realize that the alternative is far worse.

Oh, the horror of God turning His eyes away from us! It was an awful declaration of judgment when God said, "'I will hide My face from them'" (Deuteronomy 32:20). Lord, we cannot even begin to imagine such darkness! No, Lord, do not turn away from us! Even though it means the fire of Your eyes, look upon us for good. Our hearts are returning to our first prayer which we really meant all along. Look on us, visit us, come to us, O consuming fire!

I have had such sweet meditation in considering the intense concentration of God's attention upon our lives. He is more focused on me, even though I am one among billions, than I could ever be capable of reciprocating. When my mind wanders from a conscious focus upon the Lord, and I am distracted by the affairs of everyday life, upon returning to Christ in my thoughts comes this awesome realization: He was there along, waiting for my thoughts to return to Him! He is never disconnected or distracted away from me, not even for a split second. The moment my mind turns to Him, His Spirit immediately connects with my spirit and our fellowship continues, unbroken. I am in awe of this truth: He *never* stops thinking about me! His thoughts are more than the sands of the seashore (Psalm 139:18), and He knows that every one of them is for a peaceful and hopeful future (Jeremiah 29:11). Such knowledge is too wonderful for me.

"'For I will set My eyes on them for good, and I will bring them back to this land; I will build them and not pull them down, and I will plant them and not pluck them up'" (Jeremiah 24:6).

What can I say to such kindness, Lord? Here is my simple prayer: "Look upon me and be merciful to me, as Your custom is toward those who love Your name" (Psalm 119:132).

There is a place of rich affection where, in the quiet of our garden, we invoke the gaze of our Beloved. (The secret of this chapter is tucked away right here.) We have knowledge, we understand what we're saying, but we say it anyways. "Fix Your eyes on me, altogether Lovely One!" Such a resolute heart gains His extravagant response, "'You have ravished My heart, My sister, My spouse; you have ravished My heart with one look of your eyes'" (Song of Solomon 4:9). Eyes locked, hearts burning...this is the secret place.

37

The Secret of the Cross

Psalm 91:1 points directly to the cross of Jesus Christ: "He who dwells in the secret place of the Most High shall abide under the shadow of the Almighty." You can not draw closer to the shadow of God Almighty than when you are hugging the cross. *The cross's shadow is the saint's home.*

The cross is the safest place on earth. It is the place where the most violent winds will whip your soul, but also where you will enjoy the greatest immunity from Satan's devices. By embracing the cross, you are dying to every mechanism in your soul that Satan can use against you. The highest pain produces the highest freedom. There is no strategy against crucified saints because they do not love their lives even unto death.

We must return to the cross intentionally and continually. We know that we are crucified with Christ (Galatians 2:20), but self has an uncanny way of crawling off the cross and asserting itself. The crucifixion of the self-life is not an achievement but a process: We die daily (1 Corinthians 15:31). As Gethemane's garden of prayer prepared Jesus to embrace His cross, the secret place is where we reiterate our "yes" to the Father to suffer according to His will.

147

In our daily pilgrimage to the secret place, we wrap ourselves around His rugged tree, gaze upon His wounds, and once again die to ourselves. *We accept the nails in our hands that curtail our freedoms, and we surrender to the nails in our feet that immobilize us and restrict our options.* We allow the suffering of the flesh to cleanse us from sin (1 Peter 4:1). With dignity, we bear the honor of filling up in our flesh what is yet lacking with regard to the afflictions of Christ (Colossian 1:24).

Many people see the cross as the place of pain and restriction, and that is true. But it is so much more! The cross is the place of absolute love. The cross is the Father saying to the world, "This is how much I love you!" The cross is the Son saying to the Father, "This is how much I love You!" And the cross is the bride saying to her Bridegroom, "This is how much I love You!"

The cross is consummate passion poured forth. When Christ calls us to share His cross, He invites us to the highest intimacy. The wood that holds His hands now holds our hands. The nail that binds His feet to the will of God criss-crosses the nail that impales our feet to that same will. Here we hang, two lovers on opposite sides of one cross, our hearts almost touching except for the separating wood. This is our marriage bed. "Here I give to Thee my love."

As you hang with Him here, even though your vision is clouded and you cannot see His face, yet if you listen you will hear His voice. With seven words He would guide you through this dark night of your soul.

> "Father, forgive them, for they do not know what they do" (Luke 23:34).

Jesus begins by showing you the way of forgiveness toward those who have wronged you. This will be the first great hurdle you must cross, for you have truly been violated. You have been wounded in the house of your friends (Zechariah 13:6). But forgiveness is the only way you will move forward into God's purposes.

"Assuredly, I say to you, today you will be with Me in Paradise" (Luke 23:43).

While your agony is fresh and raw, the Lord assures you that your name is written in heaven, and for this alone you can rejoice. The assurance of His eternal companionship carries you in this moment.

When Jesus therefore saw His mother, and the disciple whom He loved standing by, He said to His mother, "Woman, behold your son!" Then He said to the disciple, "Behold your mother!" (John 19:26-27).

The church (represented by the woman) is actually told by Jesus to look at you in your suffering. "Behold your son!" Other believers will look upon you with reproach, misunderstanding, perplexity, and inner judgments. And then He says to you, "Behold your mother, the church." This is a time for you to look at the church and see her as you've never seen her before. You will gain great wisdom in this season if you will behold the church without any root of bitterness in your heart. What you see now will help you to serve her in times to come.

"My God, My God, why have You forsaken Me?" (Matthew 27:46).

You have just endured Jesus' three hours of silence on the cross, in the darkness. Now, Jesus directs you to this prayer of dereliction. You find yourself crying to God from the honest depths of your soul. You ask all the "why" questions. Even though you know He is so very close to you, it seems that God has forsaken you. The highest intimacy is mixed with the deepest abandonment. You do not understand why the crucible seems interminable.

"I thirst!" (John 19:28).

Rather than cursing God in your darkness, you thirst for Him and long for Him more than ever! You have come through the crucifixion and you stand at the end of it and say, "I still want You, Lord! You are my very life!"

"It is finished!" (John 19:30).

This is the moment you've been longing for, that time when Jesus would indicate that the trial is completed, finished. The work of God intended in the crucible is finally complete.

"Father, 'into Your hands I commit My spirit'" (Luke 23:46).

Jesus gently coaches you to abandon yourself completely to the hands of your beloved Father. *As you lay down your life, He takes the profound death that has worked itself in you and transforms it into resurrection life. You are joined to Christ in His death, His burial, and His resurrection!*

Unparalleled affection is reserved for those who share this cross with their Beloved. This *is* the secret place. Here exchanged are the fathomless passions of the Eternal God with His select partner. "'Greater love has no one than this, than to lay down one's life for his friends'" (John 15:13). She shares in His life, His death, and His resurrection. "For if we have been united together in the likeness of His death, certainly we also shall be in the likeness of His resurrection" (Romans 6:5). They do it all, together. Nothing can separate these two—neither death nor life nor height nor depth. Their hearts are forever entwined in the passion story of the universe. He is hers, and she is His (Song of Solomon 6:3). This is extravagant love—no length spared, no part withheld— for the cross empowers total abandonment. Every "yes" of this secret place fuels renewed exchange of exclusive devotion. Anything for love!

Come aside to the desolate hill of crucifixion. Say "yes" once more. Feel the cramping; sigh and groan. Join your suffering Savior. Drink of His cup, all of it. And discover the secret of everlasting love in the shadow of the Almighty.

I take, O cross, thy shadow
For my abiding place
I ask no other sunshine than
The sunshine of His face
Content to let the world go by
To know no gain nor loss
My sinful self my only shame
My glory all the cross.

(Elizabeth C. Clephane, Public Domain)

The Secret of Rest

And He said to them, "Come aside by yourselves to a deserted place and rest a while" (Mark 6:31).

The journey gets long for all of us. Every one of us, without exception, needs to find that place of coming aside to be refreshed in the place of rest.

Jesus said that He came to give us rest (Matthew 11:28), and yet we Christians are some of the most worn out people on the planet. Hebrews 4 clearly states there is a rest that remains for God's people, but it's very possible to miss it. God's rest is available but not guaranteed. There's something we must do to enter this rest (Hebrews 4:11).

Those who neglect the secret place always seem to struggle with stress and demands. Their lives tend toward a constant flurry of incessant activity. Jesus designed that there be a portion of our day when we just STOP. *Stop the frenetic pace, get off the merry-go-round, and calm our hearts in the love of God.*

God's rest is uncovered through a diligent pursuit of the secret place. The rest of God can be found only in ceasing from all our own works and learning to just "be" in the presence of the

Lord (Hebrews 4:10). Here is our source of rejuvenation, revitalization, invigoration, and renewal.

God instituted the Sabbath (one day of rest out of seven) for several reasons, but one of the most compelling reasons is found in Exodus 31:13, "'Speak also to the children of Israel, saying: "Surely My Sabbaths you shall keep, for it is a sign between Me and you throughout your generations, that you may know that I am the LORD who sanctifies you."'" God was saying, "When you set aside a day each week for worship and rest, you are a fragrance to me, separate (sanctified) from all the peoples of the earth. All the other peoples work hard, seven days a week, trying to get ahead and establish their lot in life. But you are different. You have faith to believe that I can bless you more in six days of labor than the heathen can glean in seven days of labor. Your honoring of the Sabbath is proof to Me that you believe in My provision, and it's a stunning garment that sets you apart from the strivings of all other peoples of the earth. Your rest in My lovingkindness makes you beautiful in My sight!"

The Sabbath is to the week as the secret place is to the day. What I mean is, even as the Sabbath was an appointed day of rest in the course of a hardworking week, the secret place is an appointed place of rest in the course of a busy day. Our commitment to the secret place sets us apart (sanctifies us) before God from the unbelieving who do not honor God at all in their day. When we take an hour to commune with our Lord and be renewed in His rest, we demonstrate our faith that God can empower us to be more effective in 23 hours of Spirit-filled service than the 24 hours that the world has without His indwelling presence.

What could be more energizing in the course of a busy day than to stop and gaze upon the glory of His enthroned majesty? Look at the effect this glorious employment has upon the living creatures in heaven's throneroom: "The four living creatures, each having six wings, were full of eyes around and within. And they do not rest day or night, saying: 'Holy, holy, holy, Lord God Almighty, who was and is and is to come!'" (Revelation 4:8). How is it that they do not rest? Are they never tired? No, they do not weary of gazing upon the beauty of the Lord for they are living in the place of eternal rejuvenation. Instead of tiring from their service to God, they are actually energized and made alive by it.

They cherish this secret, and would to God that we would learn it! It is the understanding that spending time in His presence does not diminish our productivity in life, but rather becomes the wellspring from which flows Spirit-empowered effectiveness and fruitfulness. It is the only abode of true rest.

Thank you, Lord, for providing a way for us to surrender the burdens and stresses of everyday life and be renewed in Your presence. Thank You for the privilege of burning with fiery affection before the glory of Your ineffable splendor. Thank You for the rest that empowers us to complete the marathon. Thank You, Lord, for the secret place!

Part IV

Seeking A Deeper Relationship

Secrets of the Secret Place

In Section III, we looked at secrets that will empower us to endure to the very end of the race. And now we come to the best part of this book! In this final section, we will explore valuable truths that have the potential to ignite us to new dimensions of intimacy with Christ Jesus.

The Secret of Pursuing True Riches

The Spirit of wisdom has given us the highest counsel, tucked away quietly in the book of Proverbs:

> Get wisdom! Get understanding! ...Wisdom is the principal thing; therefore get wisdom. And in all your getting, get understanding (Proverbs 4:5, 7).

Wisdom is a Spirit (Isaiah 11:2), which is why Joseph and Daniel, being full of the Spirit, evidenced such remarkable wisdom (Genesis 41:38; Daniel 5:11). And wisdom is a Person (1 Corinthians 1:30), the Lord Jesus Himself. So when we gain Christ, we gain wisdom. The pursuit of wisdom is the pursuit of Christ. Wise people are seekers of God!

What does it mean to be a person of wisdom and understanding? The answer is to be found in Psalm 14:2, "The LORD looks down from heaven upon the children of men, to see if there are any who understand, who seek God." The last two phrases of this verse are a "Hebrew parallelism," both phrases meaning the exact same thing. Thus, "any who understand" means the same thing as "any who seek God." Therefore, "to understand" means "to seek God." People of understanding seek God. Those with even half a brain will devote themselves to an abandoned pursuit of God. People who don't seek God simply don't get it. They're dull, obtuse, dim-witted, ignorant fools.

People of understanding—God seekers—have come to understand the nature of true spiritual treasure. The wise know where the "real money" is! By looking at what Jesus means by "true riches," I hope I can stir your heart to pursue the greatest riches of the kingdom.

Jesus talks about these "true riches" when He says, "'Therefore if you have not been faithful in the unrighteous mammon, who will commit to your trust the true riches?'" (Luke 16:11). In the surrounding verses, Jesus is calling His followers to responsible management of financial resources. He is saying that if we are not found faithful in our handling of unrighteous earthly money, then God will not entrust us with true riches. So the question is, what are those "true riches?" Are they positions of influence and ministry effectiveness? Are they the entrustment of oversight over eternally precious human souls? Those answers hold portions of truth, but they are not the highest answer.

The highest answer is found later on in the New Testament when Paul wrote under divine inspiration, "For it is the God who commanded light to shine out of darkness, who has shone in our hearts to give the light of the knowledge of the glory of God in the face of Jesus Christ. But we have this treasure in earthen vessels, that the excellence of the power may be of God and not of us" (2 Corinthians 4:6-7). So what is "this treasure" to which Paul refers? It is, "the light of the knowledge of the glory of God in the face of Jesus Christ." Simply put, *the treasure is the knowledge of Christ*. This is affirmed in Colossians 2:3 when Paul, speaking of Christ, wrote, "In whom are hidden all the treasures of wisdom and knowledge." So the "true riches" of Luke 16:11 are the wisdom and knowledge of Christ.

Jesus disdains earthly riches. But He extols the true eternal riches of knowing God. When we are faithful with unrighteous money, we qualify for the revelation of the beauty of the glorious Son of God, the Man Christ Jesus.

True riches are the wisdom, knowledge, and understanding of God the Father, God the Son, and God the Holy Spirit. If we have even a modicum of sense within us, we will pursue the knowledge of God with abandonment. And that's where the secret place comes in! It's here—with the word open before us, with hearts tenderized by the Spirit, and with a spiritual appetite that pants for the food of heaven—that we peer into the beauties of holiness in order to see Him more clearly and know His ways. Our souls echo the cry of Moses of long ago, "'Now therefore, I pray, if I have found grace in Your sight, show me now Your way, that I may know You and that I may find grace in Your sight'" (Exodus 33:13).

The Lord's kindness has promised, "I will give you the treasures of darkness and hidden riches of secret places, that you may know that I, the LORD, who call you by your name, am the God of Israel" (Isaiah 45:3). Originally, this was a promise to Cyrus that he would uncover the hidden treasures that were buried in Egypt's pyramids. Applied to us today, this is the Lord's assurance that there are great riches to be mined in the secret places of the Most High. Ferret out the nuggets hidden in the dark recesses of God's richly-laden word!

Faithful financial stewardship qualifies us to receive the true riches of the kingdom, but then these true riches are "bought" at the price of spending time sitting at the feet of Jesus and hearing His word.

Lord, help us to value the treasures that are hidden in You, and grant us the appetite to seek You accordingly. Give us the spirit of wisdom and revelation, that the eyes of our understanding might be enlightened, that we might know You!

40

The Secret of Beholding Jesus

S ome readers come to the Bible to gain insight or to learn truths and principles. However, coming to the Bible with your head can leave your heart untouched. There is so much more to gain from the Scriptures than truth about God. You can gain God Himself! The true riches are to be found in beholding and knowing the Lord Jesus Christ.

The Pharisees made a deadly error in how they approached the Scriptures. They dissected Scripture cognitively, but they didn't seek the heart behind the truths revealed, and thus they came to know the Book but not the Author. This is what Jesus meant when He said to them, "'You search the Scriptures, for in them you think you have eternal life; and these are they which testify of Me. But you are not willing to come to Me that you may have life'" (John 5:39-40). Everything in the Scriptures was screaming at the Pharisees, "See Jesus as you read, see Jesus!", but they missed it.

The Scriptures have always been intended to direct our hearts to a Person. Paul said that "the purpose of the commandment is love" (1 Timothy 1:5); that is, the entire purpose of the Old Testament was to enflame the hearts of God's people for the beauty of

His face. They got hung up, however, on dogma and creed and missed the living relationship that God longed to have with them.

Jesus' words to the Pharisees raise a frightening possibility: We can read the Bible avidly and never get to know the Lord. Even though Jesus is pointed to on almost every single page, it's possible to read the words and never develop a burning-heart relationship with Him. Jesus was saying we ought not come to the Scriptures to gain knowledge about a *Book*; rather, we ought to come to the Scriptures to gain knowledge about a *Person*. The Living Word desires to meet us in the Written Word, if we will but come to Him in the reading.

Here's the secret: *Your reading in the word can be a dynamic and living encounter with the person of the Lord Jesus Christ!* Don't come to the word out of a sense of rote duty to knock off your daily quota of chapters; don't come merely to master spiritual principles or to glean clever insights; come to gaze upon the majesty and mystery of the altogether Lovely One, the One who has captured your heart! He waits for you behind the veil, watching to reward those who pant and yearn for Him as for springs of living water. Come with a cry in your heart to see Him and know Him. With a tiny breath of His Spirit on a single word of Scripture, He can set your heart racing with fresh revelation of His power and glory.

When Jesus joined up with the two disciples on the road to Emmaus after His resurrection, He began to explain to them how He was the central theme of the Scriptures. Imagine the glory of this encounter—Jesus revealing Jesus to the human spirit from the written word! Little wonder that those disciples later recalled, "'Did not our heart burn within us while He talked with us on the road, and while He opened the Scriptures to us?'" (Luke 24:32). It's the opening of the Scriptures concerning Christ to the thirsty soul, through the power of the Holy Spirit, that gives the burning heart. This is the great pursuit of the secret place!

Jesus chided the Sadducees with this indictment, "'You are mistaken, not knowing the Scriptures nor the power of God'" (Matthew 22:29). This suggestions three sad possibilities:

- We can know the Scriptures but not the power of God.
- We can know the power of God but not the Scriptures.
- We can know neither the Scriptures nor the power of God.

My heart cries out, "I want to know *You*, Lord! I want to behold You in Your Scriptures. I want to know You and the fullness of Your power! Manifest Yourself to me in Your word, O my Lord!" It is because of this heart-cry that I run into the secret place. I long for Him so much that I am lovesick with unfulfilled desires. "Oh, when will You come to me?"

My experience has been that I don't get to know Jesus better in prayer. Prayer is where I express my love according to how I have come to know Him. Prayer is love exchanged. *But if I am to come to know Him better, I must approach His word and behold Him there. To know more of Christ requires revelation, and revelation usually requires meditation in the word.* "But we all, with unveiled face, beholding as in a mirror the glory of the Lord, are being transformed into the same image from glory to glory, just as by the Spirit of the Lord" (2 Corinthians 3:18).

Oh, how we long to behold Him! I consider, with a certain kind of envy, the living creatures who do not turn from facing straight ahead no matter where they go (Ezekiel 1:12-17). Whether they go up or down, left or right, forward or backwards, their faces are constantly facing straight forward—at the throne! They have the glorious privilege of ever gazing upon the beauty of the King. Lord, this is how I want to live my life, too. That no matter where I go and what I do, my face might be fastened upon the throne and beholding the radiance of my beloved Lord.

The more I see of Jesus in His word, the more I realize that He is nothing like me. But when I see Him in His uniqueness, this is the very thing that draws me most passionately into His heart. I've discovered that I am naturally attracted to that which is different from me (as the saying goes, opposites attract). Jesus is stunning in His singular beauty and matchless majesty. And oh, what a privilege I have—to come to the secret place and gaze upon Him in the Scriptures, forever fascinated with the adventure of growing in the knowledge of Him who died for me!

41

The Secret of Standing

When you retreat to the secret place, you are standing in the Spirit together with all the saints on the sea of glass and gazing upon the One who is seated on the throne (Revelation 15:2). Even though your eyes are veiled so you can't see Him with the natural eye, you are still standing directly before the throne! The highest privilege of all creation is to stand before the living fire of God's presence and burn with holy affections for your Father and King. Standing here is your eternal destiny, and you can taste a bit of heaven on earth by shutting your door and standing before your God in the beauty of holiness.

Your schedule doesn't want to let you stand here; work demands militate against you standing here; hells wars against you standing here. But you are awakened to the beauties of holiness, and now you long to come aside and stand in His presence. Just to stand; and having done all, to stand!

To stand, despite the warfare; to stand, despite the resistance; to stand, despite the hassles; to stand, despite the weariness; to stand, despite the distresses; to stand, despite the temptations; to stand, despite personal failure and collapse; to stand, despite the grief; to stand, despite the loneliness; to stand, even when chained; just to stand!

To stand, because of the cross; to stand, because of the Lamb; to stand, because of His affections; to stand, because of His acceptance; to stand, because of His mighty power within; to stand, because of fountains of living water flowing up from the innermost being; to stand, because of His surpassing beauty and greatness; to stand, because of His eternal purpose; to stand, because of His everlasting mercies; to stand, because of love; just to stand!

The job description for the Levites is still applicable to us today: "At that time the LORD separated the tribe of Levi to bear the ark of the covenant of the LORD, to stand before the LORD to minister to Him and to bless in His name, to this day" (Deuteronomy 10:8). *One of our prime responsibilities (and privileges!) is to stand before the Lord to minister to Him.* In the secret place we simply stand. No great agenda, no mighty ambitions, no rush to move on to the next thing. We just stand before Him and love Him.

There are seasons when God calls us to simply stand. We might prefer the adrenalin of chasing down a great cause, but sometimes God calls us to stop all activity and just stand. Sometimes He gives us no choice. Occasionally, circumstances will constrain us beyond our ability to steer a different course, and we become prisoners to the chains that bind us to God's will. Incapable of extricating ourselves and moving on to the next thing, all we can do is stand and burn in holy love for our King.

It is commonly said, "Don't just *stand* there, *do* something!" When circumstances in our lives are careening out of control, the great temptation—when you don't know what to do—is to do *something*. "God can't steer a stationary vehicle," they say, "So start moving out on *something*, and let God direct your course."

That may be the way to go in some situations, but I've found that the Lord has been working differently in my life in recent days. He inverted that common saying and gave it to me this way, "Don't just *do* something, *stand* there!" It came like this: "When you don't know what to do, don't just do *something!* Wait on Me, stand before Me, minister to Me, until. Until I speak. When I speak to you, then you can move out in response. But until I speak, just stand there."

So like the Levites of old (Deuteronomy 10:8), I bear His presence on my shoulders, I stand before Him to minister to Him, and I bless others in His name as He strengthens me. "I have set the LORD always before me" (Psalm 16:8). So I will stand before Him, gaze upon His beauty, and bless Him while I have my breath.

To stand before God in this way, we can learn something from the angels. For example, look at Gabriel. When the angel Gabriel came to tell Zecharias that he would father John the Baptist, it was Gabriel's second appearance in Scripture. Actually, Garbriel is seen three times in the Bible. He appeared the first time to Daniel, and then almost 600 years later he visited Zecharias, and then he came to Mary six months later to announce her impregnation by the Holy Spirit. When Gabriel came to Zecharias with God's message, Zecharias did not believe his words. In response to Zecharias's unbelief, Gabriel rose up to reinforce the certainty of his message by declaring, "'I am Gabriel, who stands in the presence of God'" (Luke 1:19).

"So what do you do, Gabriel?" we might ask.

"I stand in the presence of God."

"Yes, we understand that, but what do you do?"

"Actually, I stand in the presence of God."

"Yes, yes, Gabriel, we understand that! But what we're asking is, what do you *do*??"

Gabriel would say, "That's what I do! I stand in the presence of God. I stand there, beholding His majesty and splendor, burning with His holy flame, and wait upon Him until He speaks. If He says nothing, I just stand there. When He gives me a word, then I move out to fulfill it. But mostly what I do is I just stand before God and wait on Him."

Between Daniel and Zecharias is a 600-year period during which we hear nothing from Gabriel; then between Zecharias and Mary was a 6-month period. That was the busy season! What did Gabriel do between assignments? He just stood there.

I've discovered that sometimes God is wasteful. He watches while you cultivate your gifts and talents and ministry abilities, until you become a finely tuned piece of ministry potential. You're ready to do exploits! And then He takes the well-oiled ministry machine that you've become and places you on the shelf—and He says, "Just stand there."

This is what God did with Elijah. Elijah had this expression, "'As the LORD God of Israel lives, before whom I stand'" (1 Kings 17:1). Elijah claimed, "I stand before God, that's what I do." So the Lord decided to test his claim by putting him under house arrest for three years. In the widow's home during the famine, he couldn't stick his head out the door because every nation on earth was looking for him. He was stuck in this hot, stuffy, bleak little house. No friends, no visiting prophets, no other voices to comfort or give him perspective. And the food? Frycakes for breakfast, frycakes for lunch, and more of the same for supper. I can imagine Elijah thinking, "Lord, why do You have all this ministry potential holed up in this widow's house? I mean, in the last three years I could have raised up a whole graduating class in the School Of The Prophets. We would be taking the nations by force! But no, here I stand and rot!" But Elijah didn't respond that way because God had already taught him to stand before Him. So when the time of testing came, Elijah was able to persevere and just stand before His God and minister to Him.

The Scriptures show us that God has mighty angels who stand in His presence, in some cases for hundreds of years, and wait for His bidding. With all their strength and might, God just has them standing around the throne and waiting on Him! If it were a matter of strength, God has all the strength in heaven He needs! And then the Holy Spirit whispered to me, "I don't need your strength." It wasn't the strength of the eternal Son that bought our redemption; it was the fact that He was crucified in weakness that brought us salvation. God doesn't need our strength; He needs our availability. *He's just looking for us to stand in His presence, gaze upon Him, love Him, and fulfill His word when He speaks.*

Are you between assignments? Then just stand before Him, enjoy Him, and let Him enjoy you!

The Secret of Bodily Light

We know that Jesus came to give us light in our spirit, soul, and understanding. Please consider with me, though, the truth that He also came to give us light in our *body*. Here's where Jesus talked about it:

> "No one, when he has lit a lamp, puts it in a secret place or under a basket, but on a lampstand, that those who come in may see the light. The lamp of the body is the eye. Therefore, when your eye is good, your whole body also is full of light. But when your eye is bad, your body also is full of darkness. Therefore take heed that the light which is in you is not darkness. If then your whole body is full of light, having no part dark, the whole body will be full of light, as when the bright shining of a lamp gives you light" (Luke 11:33-36).

It's fascinating that Jesus spoke of our bodies as though they can be filled with either light or darkness. The implications of this truth are vitally important to our victory and joy in Christ, and intensely relevant to our secret place. I have only a tiny bit of insight into this truth, so I hope in this chapter that I might whet your appetite to search it out further.

167

There is a place in God where our bodies are full of light, where all darkness has been eradicated from our bodies. This is a place of incredible freedom from temptation. Temptation often finds its power in the fact that it is able to appeal to dark areas within our body. *When the body is full of light, bodily sins lose their power over us, and we walk in a fantastic dimension of victory.* (When I speak of bodily sins I am referring to sins that we commit with our bodies, such as drunkenness, gluttony, fornication, masturbation, viewing pornography, illegal drug usage, murder, stealing, lying, slander, coarse language, etc.)

How do we get greater light into our body? Jesus clearly taught that light comes to the body through the eye. A good eye will bring light into the body; a bad eye will keep light out. The whole thing has to do with the eyes.

If we come to the secret place with a clear and healthy eye, the light of God's word will penetrate every facet of our lives, our bodies included, and we will become filled with light in every part of our being. It is vitally important what we look at! If we peer into the law of liberty (God's word), we will be filled with illumination and clarity; if we look at things that defile, we not only fill our minds with garbage, but we also allow darkness to get established in portions of our body.

Guard your eyes, dearly beloved! Give your eyes to reading His word and beholding His face. Then, when temptation comes, your body will not be fighting against your spirit. Your body will be in alignment with the light, and the tentacles of lust and greed and anger will not be able to wrap around and enslave you.

I was reading a Christian magazine awhile ago in which a reader was writing about his struggles with his thought life. He was crying for help to know how to do battle against lust. The editor's glib response was basically, "Lighten up; you're too hard on yourself. There are healthy ways to enjoy beautiful women without wanting them." I was dumbfounded. The editor's offhanded response didn't even begin to equip the brother for warfare against his inner torment. How I could have wished for this brother to hear, "Check your eyes! What are you looking at? Are you spending time gazing into the word of God that you might fill your body with light?"

When our eye is bad, we can come to God's word and still not see anything. We must do more than stop looking at the wrong things—we must put salve on our eyes so that we might see the right things. "'Anoint your eyes with eye salve, that you may see'" (Revelation 3:18). What is this eye salve? I believe the salve Jesus referred to is the application of the spiritual disciplines in our lives—fasting, prayer, study of Scripture, almsgiving, forgiveness, etc. "The commandment of the LORD is pure, enlightening the eyes" (Psalm 19:8). *As we apply ourselves to God's word in a disciplined, focused way, our eye will slowly begin to heal and clear up and will begin to allow the light of Christ into our bodies.*

But victory over sin is not the greatest reward of a body filled with light. Of far greater significance is the intimacy we find with Christ! When our body is filled with light, our body has come into full alignment with God's kingdom and purposes. There is nothing within our bodies that is resisting His will. This dimension of cooperation with God's purposes greatly strengthens our sense of "sweet sincerity" before the Lord, and the soul gains great confidence in the Lord's embrace. Without impediment, you are now a clear channel of grace.

When you come to worship the Lord with a body full of light, you don't need a "warm up" period before you finally engage with God. No, you are on "constant hot"; you are continually "fervent in spirit" (Romans 12:11); you are ready at a moment's notice to soar in the Spirit with your Beloved.

The Lord began the teaching on bodily light by stating how He handles those whose bodies are filled with light. He said, "'No one, when he has lit a lamp, puts it in a secret place or under a basket, but on a lampstand, that those who come in may see the light'" (Luke 11:33). Jesus was saying when our eye is good and our whole body is full of light, we begin to shine with a radiance beyond what we may even realize. We're ablaze with truth, like a shining lamp! The Lord says when He has set you on fire with that kind of light, He will not bury your life in a place of obscurity and hiddenness. No, He will place that kind of light on a lampstand, "'that those who come in may see the light.'"

When your body is filled with light, you will know greater victory over bodily sins, you will touch deeper dimensions of intimacy with Jesus, and you will be granted a place of greater influence in the body of Christ. Oh, this is a powerful secret! Put a guard on your eyes! Reserve them for beholding the glory of God and looking into His wonderful word. Then your entire being will radiate the light and glory of God!

43

The Secret of Just Loving Him

G od gave His only begotten Son, and Jesus died an excruciating death, all for love. The central reason for this whole thing between God and man is love! He didn't die to enlist your strength in His army; He already has all the power He needs to vanquish every foe. He didn't die for you because He was lonely and looking for companionship, for He is surrounded in glory by multiplied millions of creatures. He didn't die for you because He was bored and had nothing better to do. *He died for one all-encompassing reason, that He might manifest the graciousness of His glorious love to us, and in turn reap the extravagant affections of a lovesick bride. He did it all for love.*

Love is the primary staple of the secret place. So you'll often find yourself spending most of your quiet time in the simple exchange of affection. You'll find a thousand and more ways to say, "I love You," and He'll amaze you with the creativity and energy with which He'll reciprocate His passions for you.

Start your day with just loving Him. Your requests can wait; your Bible studying can wait; your intercessions can wait. Before anything else, give your love to your Lord. Let Him know that love is the great motivator of your heart. "I'm here, Father, because I love You. You are the center of my universe! I hallow and reverence Your name. I enjoy being with You."

The Lord has put His requirements within easy reach of every one of us, regardless of social class, age, personality, giftings, etc. All He asks for is love. Even the mentally handicapped are usually capable of loving. Love is the great equalizer in the kingdom, putting us all on the same playing field. No one has an advantage over another in giving and receiving love.

Don't come to Jesus and try to be intellectually stimulating to Him. There's nothing you could say that would cause Him to respond, "Wow, that's a neat insight!" You may as well abort all attempts to be cerebral with Jesus; He simply doesn't try to engage us at that level. Just come and love Him. He's looking for heartfelt sincerity, for visceral passion, for authentic relationship. No matter what kind of a dullard you think you might be, you can love. And He loves you! He enjoys all of us equally when we just love Him.

The secret place is where we seek to become a better lover of God. We practice the language of love; we surrender to the Spirit of love; we search for ways to give even more of our hearts to Him in love. This has nothing to do with your personality. No matter how emotional or non-emotional your temperament, you can love. And you can get better at it. "Lord, give me a childlike simplicity that delights in your simplest blessings."

The times I enjoy my kids most are when they are enjoying my company or expressing their affection to me. When they do so, it's never with fancy words or careful decorum. They might even be clumsy or unsure of how to express themselves. It might be the simplest expression, or maybe just a kiss without any words whatsoever, but it melts my heart. Lord, grant me the freedom to be childlike in Your presence.

As you express your love to the Lord, you may find yourself instinctively wanting to sing to Him. That's what the secret place is all about! *It's the place where you can express yourself to your Friend without inhibition, knowing that He doesn't get distracted with your pitch or vibrato or rhythmic meter; He looks straight at your heart and receives your song as though it were the finest solo.* There's an intrinsic bond between music and love. Listen to a radio station, and you'll discover that 95% of the world's songs have to do with love. Music and love go together. That's why music and singing are such a natural part of our secret life with God. Let the Spirit carry you away on the winds of worship, open the inner chambers of your soul, and sing in the Spirit to your Beloved (Ephesians 5:19). Learn to soar in the song of the Lord!

As Christ dwells in our hearts through faith, we are rooted and grounded in love (Ephesians 3:17). As you give yourself to loving your Lord, you are putting down roots into the love of God. It's the confidence of His love for you that will carry you through the storms of life. Satan wants to blow you over with the winds of adversity, but you have become established and rooted in love as you have pursued a living relationship with Christ through faith. Nothing can unsettle you because you are now established in love. Even though the love of many will grow cold (Matthew 24:12), it will not come near you, for you are rooted in a love that will never let you go.

Oh, dear friend, are you established in the Father's love? As His word is open before you, and as you give your heart to Him, let Him begin to lavish upon you the infinite riches of His eternal love. He loves you with an everlasting love (Jeremiah 31:3)! He has literally killed Himself to be one with you. His love is so breathtaking and intoxicating that when you are filled with this love, the Scriptures testify that you are being filled with all the fullness of God Himself (Ephesians 3:16-19). What a glorious adventure, to explore the magnificent recesses of the boundless love of Christ!

One of the most powerful assurances that I carry in my heart is Psalm 91:14, "Because he has set his love upon Me, therefore I will deliver him." I have chosen to set my love upon Him every day, regardless of circumstances, because I know that He is working even the difficult circumstances together for good. As I come to the secret place and daily set my affections upon Him, I am established in the confidence that He will deliver me.

I remember a five-year period of darkness during which all I could do was fall on my face before the Lord and say, "I love You."

I couldn't do any spiritual warfare; I couldn't do any intercession; I couldn't fight any battles. All I could do was love. In retrospect, I now realize I was exercising the most powerful form of warfare possible. Love is the most powerful force in the universe. *When you simply release your love to your Lord, you are stepping into the dimension where God works on behalf of His loved ones.* I hope you're latching onto this awesome secret. Just love Him! Open the alabaster jar of your heart and pour yourself upon His feet in loving adoration. You'll unlock the passions of heaven and be lifted into new dimensions of blessed communion with your Lover and Friend.

The Secret of Being Known

Someone once asked, "Do you know God?" But there's a question that is far more important: Does God know you? The issue on the great day of judgment will not be whether you know God but whether God knows you.

Many will claim to know God in the day of judgment. They will say to Him, "Lord, Lord, I know You! I have prophesied in Your name, cast out demons in Your name and done many wonders in Your name. I ate and drank in Your presence, and You taught in our streets. I swear I *do* know You!"

But to some of them He will reply, "I don't know you, and I don't know where you're from. In fact, I *never* knew you. Depart from Me, you who practice lawlessness!" (See Matthew 7:21-23 and Luke 13:25-27.)

No words could possibly be more terrifying to hear! How horrifying to *think* you know God, only to discover that He doesn't know you! The issues at risk here are of eternal consequence. There can be no more fundamentally important question than this: What must I do to be known by God?

The answer has everything to do with my secret life with God. *He wants me to enter the secret place, sit before Him, remove every façade and mask of pretense, and reveal to Him the innermost secrets of my heart.* He wants me to unveil my face before Him (2 Corinthians 3:18) and let Him see the real me. The good, the bad, the ugly—all of it. He wants me to love Him without withholding any part of my being. He wants a relationship with me that is based in total transparency and honesty. I am changing more and more into the image of Christ, but during the process I allow Him to see the naked truth of my brokenness and carnality.

"But," someone might counter, "I thought God knows everything about us anyways!"

True, He does. But just because He sees certain dark rooms in our hearts doesn't mean we've invited His light into those dark rooms. The human tendency is to hide and cover up. If we try to hide our true condition from Him, not only do we deceive ourselves, but we also hold ourselves back from being known by Him. When He says He knows us, He means that we have invited Him into every part of our thoughts, motives, desires, and actions. When we invite Him in, He releases His grace to empower us to overcome sinful patterns that had previously seemed unconquerable.

Judas Iscariot serves as a compelling example of a man who was incredibly close to Jesus but yet didn't allow Jesus into the secrets of his heart. He had a major problem with stealing, but He refused to confess it and bring it into the light. Jesus gave him multiple opportunties over a three-year period to open up, but Judas repeatedly chose to hide, hide, hide. Eventually Satan was able to reach into that stronghold in Judas's life and yank him to his destruction. *Judas illustrates the terrifying truth that it's possible to spend lots of time in the presence of Jesus and still not be known by Him.*

Jesus can handle the confessions of our actual struggles; what He can't handle is when we hide them and pretend they don't exist. The secret place is no place for secrets. It's the place for total honesty and full disclosure. When we reveal our struggles, He releases the grace to help us change. This is how we let Him know who we really are.

Now here's the awesome part: When we confess our struggles to Him, He lavishes us with acceptance and ownership. He says, "Since you're willing to show Me your inner ugliness, I am willing to confess you before My Father and claim you as My own!" Wow! I feared that He might reject me if He knew the real me; as it turns out, He accepts me when I let Him see the real me. His grace truly is amazing! *His acceptance is so incredible that it inspires me to open every single crevice of my heart to His loving eyes.*

And *that's* where the intimacy is! The greatest intimacy is found in the mutual giving of ourselves radically to each other. The cross demonstrates how radically He gives Himself to me, and my embracing of the cross is my giving myself back to Him with lavish abandonment. Not only am I honest with Him; I search for ways to give even *more* of my heart to Him. It's the search for increasing self-disclosure that causes my relationship with Him to be deepened and enriched.

Someone once said, "Prayer demands a relationship in which you allow someone other than yourself to enter into the very center of your being, to see there what you would rather leave in darkness, and to touch there what you would rather leave untouched" (author unknown).

Isn't it great to be truly known by Him? As Bill Gaither penned the song, "The one who knows me best loves me most!" He knows me, and He understands me.

One reason we find such delight in surrendering our lives to Christ's leadership is because He never misunderstands us. All of us have known the frustration of feeling or thinking one way about a certain issue, but having someone else totally misinterpret our thoughts or intentions and thus judge us wrongly. That never happens with Jesus. He always knows exactly what we're thinking and what is motivating us. This is one reason the twelve disciples found Jesus' leadership so compelling—because He was able to address the issues of their hearts with total accuracy and complete understanding. He knew them like an open book, and His ability to provide compassionate leadership in the power of that knowledge endeared them to Him forever. They felt

177

completely understood, even when they were wrong and being rebuked for it. Jesus both knew them implicitly and loved them unconditionally. Oh, the blessedness of being known by God!

How can we be known by God? The answer is given to us most simply in 1 Corinthians 8:3, "But if anyone loves God, this one is known by Him." When we open our hearts to Him in loving abandonment, He embraces us and knows us. What a joyful privilege—to have a knowing relationship with God Almighty! Thank you, Jesus, for the gift of the secret place where we can give each other this love.

45

The Secret of Intimacy First

The first thing is the greatest thing: to love God with all one's being. It's the greatest commandment (Matthew 22:37-38), and it's the first thing in our lives (Revelation 2:4). Intimacy with God must be our first priority before anything else, even before our works of service. The second commandment (loving others, which are our works of service) "is like" the first commandment, according to Jesus, and yet Jesus clearly called it "second" (Matthew 22:39). It's an extremely close second and difficult to separate from the first, and yet it is second.

It's vitally important that we keep first things first. When our love for God gets our first and best attention, then we will function in the spiritual wholeness necessary to execute the second commandment. When our priorities become inverted and we begin placing more emphasis on loving others than loving God, we are headed for certain burnout. The only way to avoid an eventual collapse is to keep returning to our first love.

The Holy Spirit is profoundly committed to restoring the first commandment to first place in our lives. We must be established in our primary identity before God. It's so important to be able to say, "This is who I am." I am not primarily a worker for

God; I am first and foremost a lover of God. The Holy Spirit is visiting many of us in this hour and turning the tables of our priorities and understandings upsidedown. His mandate is to establish our primary identity as lovers of God. *By the time He is finished in our lives, we will be lovers who work rather than workers who love.*

The secret place must have top priority in our calendars and schedules because it is the place where the incubation of intimacy is facilitated. You can't garner intimacy on the run. You must stop, pull up a table, lay out the bread and the cup, and dine with Him and He with you. It's great to enjoy His presence while driving to work in the morning, but if your commute to work is the totality of your secret place, then you will lack depth of connection in your intimacy with Jesus. The responses of His heart are lavishly explosive when we give Him our first and best energies.

Speaking from personal experience, I know what it's like to get the two greatest commandments inverted without even realizing it. There came a time when the Lord pulled me up short and in His kindness showed me how my life priorities were imbalanced. He said, "Bob, you come to Me like to a gas station." Now, I consider a gas station to be a "necessary evil." I don't like to fill up with gas, I like to drive. But I know that if I'm going to do what I *really* want to do (drive), then I've got to fill up with gas. The Lord was saying, "Bob, you come to the place of prayer in order to get filled up. You don't come to Me because I'm the first love of your heart; you come to Me to get recharged so that you can go out and pursue the first love of your life." You see, my first love was the ministry. I loved to drive! I wanted to see souls saved; I wanted to win my city for Christ; I wanted to change the world. I was motivated more by what I did for God than by being with Him. I claimed, "All my springs are in You" (Psalm 87:7), but in fact what sustained me most was the "rush" of ministry accomplishments. And I didn't even realize it until the Lord showed it to me.

When I saw this, I went into writhing pain. I fell before Him and cried, "Lord, I'm sorry, this isn't how I want it to be. I don't want to have a filling station relationship with You! I want so much more! I want to be Your lover, Your bride. I want You to be the number one love of my life. I want the secret place to be what I live for. I want to enjoy being with You so much that they have to drag me out of the secret place!"

I sensed the Lord responding, "Yes, son, I know that's what you want. And that's why I've come to you and shown you the true condition of your heart. I'm going to allure you into the wilderness (Hosea 2), and there I will awaken you to a depth of love relationship beyond anything you've known in your young and busy years."

The Lord has many ways to bring us to proper priorities. In my case, He simply removed my ministry. Oh how it hurt! I cried out, "Lord, why does this hurt so much? You haven't removed Your presence from my life; all You've done is remove my ministry. And I am in incalculable pain. Why does it hurt so much?" It was in this way that the Lord showed me how much the ministry had become the fountain of my soul. When He removed it, I was granted an opportunity to find an entirely new basis for relating with Him. I began to learn what it means to come to Him simply for the joy and delight of who He is.

He doesn't remove everybody's ministry in order to teach them this valuable lesson. In same cases, He simply starves out our fulfillment in our labors for Him. We're still doing the same ministry, but it no longer fulfills us. The ministry becomes dry, dusty, lifeless, and laborious. We find ourselves dreading what once energized us. It's the same net effect: the Lord is trying to show us how we have derived sustenance from our works of service instead of from the kisses of His mouth.

He wants us addicted to the wine of His love (Song of Solomon 1:2), but it's so easy to become addicted to the wine of ministry. Ministry can be intoxicating. There is a certain "high" that happens when the grace of God flows through you and ministers to the bride. When her face lights up with the glory of God, you feel a sense of fulfillment and significance because God honored your obedience and blessed others. Furthermore, you had the privilege of watching God use the gifts and talents you've cultivated.

181

Your inner response is like, "This is it! This is what I was created for! I've found my niche. This is my calling and ministry. Now I know my place in the body. Serving in this way is giving me such a wonderful feeling that I want to do it again!" It's not wrong to enjoy ministering to others, but it's so easy for this to become the addictive wine that intoxicates and fulfills us, and the wine of His love takes second place to this "new wine" we've tasted called ministry.

So the Lord comes to us, like He did to the Ephesians who were so successful in ministry, and He says, "I'm calling you back to your first love" (see Revelation 2:4). *He wants us to be people of "one thing": the passionate pursuit of His face.* David said, "One thing I have desired of the LORD, that will I seek: that I may dwell in the house of the LORD all the days of my life, to behold the beauty of the LORD, and to inquire in His temple" (Psalm 27:4). David chased after *"one thing"*—the face of God; Paul said, "But *one thing* I do"—which was the pursuit of "the upward call of God in Christ Jesus" (Philippians 3:13-14); Mary of Bethany discovered that, *"One thing* is needed," and Jesus added that she had "chosen that good part, which will not be taken away from her" (Luke 10:42). There's only *one thing* that is really necessary, and that is to sit at Jesus' feet and hear His words. David's one thing was Paul's one thing was Mary's one thing. *It's the first commandment in first place, the pursuit of a loving relationship with our dazzling Bridegroom.*

All of hell will militate against your becoming a man or woman of one thing. Circumstances will go haywire; your to-do list will mushroom; the demands on your life will escalate. Satan will employ whatever device will work—anything to keep you from becoming a person of one thing. Because if you find this attainment, you will become a passionate firebrand for God, set ablaze with fiery bridal passions for your Lord, and you will be a dangerous weapon in the hand of your God for endtime exploits. The greatest dimensions of kingdom power will be touched by those who are truly ignited and energized by their personal love relationship with the Lord Jesus.

Ask yourself this question: Am I ever relieved when my prayer time is over? For me the answer was, "More times than I care to admit!" There were so many times I was relieved to be finished with the filling-up process so that I could go out and drive the machinery of my ministry. But the Lord has been kind to me, and He is teaching me the secret of loving Him first and deriving my fulfillment and sense of success from the affections He gives me in the secret place. When I'm a success in His arms, the ministry can go well, or it can go not so well; I'm a success on the inside either way. Thus I am stabilized by the power of an inner life with God, rather than being jerked around emotionally by the vicissitudes of the ministry's ups and downs.

In closing, look at Matthew 5:15, "'Nor do they light a lamp and put it under a basket, but on a lampstand, and it gives light to all who are in the house.'" The Lord wants to set you ablaze with zeal for the face of Christ so that you might shine with the light of a relationship that enjoys intimacy first. If this fire of love is pure and bright, the Lord will set you on a lampstand so that you might give light to the entire household of faith. But if the light of your life isn't pure—if it's energized in part by the wine of ministry—then the Lord will place your light under a basket. *Some of the most gifted ministries have been placed under a basket and been limited to a localized sphere of influence because the Lord was not willing to export the impurity of their love to the entire body of Christ.* May you learn the secret of loving Jesus first and foremost, that He might see fit to place your lamp on a lampstand and make the simplicity and purity of your devotion an example to the greater household of faith. Amen.

46

The Secret of Bridal Identity

One day as I was driving down the highway at about 50 m.p.h., I noticed two turtledoves standing in the road ahead of me. (Turtledoves usually are seen in pairs as they mate for life.) I thought to myself, "Those birds better get off the road or I'll hit them." Sure enough, by the time they started to move it was too late, and THWAP!! There were feathers everywhere. I hit them both. I thought to myself, "Stupid birds. They should have moved sooner." It was later I learned something about doves: they have no peripheral vision. They can only see straight ahead. The poor birds didn't even see me coming! By the time they saw me, it was too late.

The heavenly Bridegroom likens us to a dove when He says, "You have dove's eyes'" (Song of Solomon 1:15). To Him, we are a like a turtledove that lacks peripheral vision. So here's what your Lord says to you, His bride: "You have dove's eyes. You have tunnel vision for Me only. You're not distracted with other affections and desires to the right or the left. Your gaze is upon Me only, and I love that!" You are His bride, and you have eyes for One only, your Beloved.

Here are two of the many places where the Bible refers to God's people as a bride:

Then I, John, saw the holy city, New Jerusalem, coming down out of heaven from God, *prepared as a bride adorned for her husband* (Revelation 21:2).

Then one of the seven angels who had the seven bowls filled with the seven last plagues came to me and talked with me, saying, "Come, I will show you *the bride, the Lamb's wife*" (Revelation 21:9).

The bridal imagery of a cosmic wedding appears frequently throughout the entire Bible, starting in the beginning with Adam and Eve and ending with the last chapter of the Bible. The message is very clear and consistent: *We are the bride of Christ, being prepared for a great wedding celebration in the age to come, when we will be joined forever in great affection to our Bridegroom, the Lord Jesus Christ.*

Believers fulfill the feminine role in the relationship as we commune with our Lord. He initiates, we respond; He gives, we receive; He impregnates, we bring to birth; He leads, we follow; He loves, we reciprocate; He rules, we reign with Him. Men who struggle with seeing themselves as a bride should remember that the sisters among us must also see themselves as sons of God. The Bible calls us both a bride and sons because both images point in an incomplete way to the beauty of the perfection to which we are called. We relate to the Father as sons; we relate to the Lord Jesus as a bride.

Generally, the sisters have an easier time with the secret of this chapter—learning to relate to Jesus as His lovesick bride. But the brothers can gain this secret, too. New dimensions of intimacy and responsiveness open to us when we embrace our bridal identity and relate to Jesus as our Bridegroom.

When Jesus looks at us, clothed in white garments of righteousness, replete with good works, mature in affections, making ourselves ready for our wedding day, His ravished heart soars with delight and desire for His espoused virgin, His bride. He can hardly wait till that day—neither can we! In the meantime, we court each other with love, attention, words of affection, honor, and delight. The secret place is the king's chamber (Song of Solomon 1:4), the place where we nurture our growing love relationship.

This is where He speaks over us, declaring how beautiful and fair we are in His sight. We respond by opening our hearts to Him with greater abandonment, praising the glorious attributes of His beauty and character, and receiving the lavish affections of His heart. Oh, the exchange of love in the secret place is most glorious! He sure knows how to capture a heart and keep it!

Jesus didn't die to marry "amazon woman," a battle axe of a bride that is so tough that she intimidates with her hulking strength and imposing demeanor. Nor did He die to marry a work-horse who will tirelessly labor to fulfill His household chores and glean His fields. He died for love. *He died to marry a beautiful bride who will walk with Him, talk with Him, dream with Him, laugh with Him, strategize with Him, and rule with Him.*

When my bride came walking down the aisle toward me many years ago, all dressed in white, with a glow about her face, let me tell you what I was *not* thinking. I was *not* thinking. "She's got good teeth. She bakes a mean pie. She cooks great food. She'll do my laundry for me. She'll change the diapers for my kids. She'll keep my house clean." Here's what I *was* thinking: "Here comes my lover!" Yes, when we got married, Marci knew that she would manage our home and rear our children and prepare meals and do laundry; but we didn't get married for any of those reasons. We got married for love.

It's true that we're soldiers, and we are involved in high-level strategic warfare, and the Lord is depending on us to fight the good fight of faith. And it's true that we're laborers in His vineyard, working assiduously in the harvest fields to bring all of the wheat into His barn. But Jesus didn't die to win for Himself an army or a labor force; He died for a bride. We don't come to the secret place as a soldier looking for battle plans, even though He will unfold His plans to us while we're there; nor do we come as laborers looking to gain strength for the day's labors, even though He will strengthen us for the tasks before us. We come primarily as His bride, to enjoy His embrace and to lavish upon Him our love. *The secret place is a celebration of our highest identity—His bride!* It's the place of intimate love exchange.

The apostle John was shown the cry that would grip believers at the end of the age: "And the Spirit and the bride say, 'Come!' And let him who hears say, 'Come!' And let him who thirsts come. Whoever desires, let him take the water of life freely" (Revelation 22:17). Although many metaphors are used for God's people—e.g., we are His body, His temple, an army, etc.—the last metaphor that the Bible uses to reveal our identity is that of "the bride." I believe this is a prophetic declaration that at the end of the age God's people will come into a fuller ownership of their identity as the bride of Christ. While every image has its limitations, the most complete metaphor of our identity is that of the bride. Jesus is returning for a bride consumed with bridal affections for her beloved Bridegroom!

Knowing that a bride and bridegroom just love to be together, let me ask you a question. Do you ever waste time with the Lord? When I ask that question, I'm thinking of Mary of Bethany who lavished her inheritance (the costly flask of fragrant oil) upon the Lord, and was reviled by the disciples with the words, "Why this waste?" (Matthew 26:8). They viewed her effusive display of love as wasteful. But Jesus validated her love, establishing the truth that it is fitting at times to be wasteful by extravagantly pouring ourselves out upon Him. So again, do you ever waste time with the Lord? What I mean is, after you have done your Bible reading, and after you have praised and worshiped, after you have presented your requests and interceded, and after you have been filled and renewed in the Holy Spirit, do you ever spend just a little more time with Him only for the sake of love? You don't "need" to spend any more time in the secret place for your own sake, but you choose to stay there just to "waste" some time in His presence for His sake—because you're a lovesick bride, and you just long to be with Him. What dignity and honor the Lord Jesus has ascribed to those who choose to waste their lives and love on Him.

Many of us live with feelings of guilt regarding the secret place because we lose focus on our identity as Christ's bride.

Spending time with Him is not an obligation or a duty; it's the thrill and longing of our soul. When we're able to be with Him, we're overjoyed; when other tasks pull us away from that companionship, we feel only a sense of loss and frustration. And an even keener anticipation of our next time together! The secret place is not where we perform our sacred duty as a believer but where we revel in the delight of being with the One our soul loves.

Look with me at how the bride of Christ is described in her fullness: "And he who talked with me had a gold reed to measure the city, its gates, and its wall. The city is laid out as a square; its length is as great as its breadth. And he measured the city with the reed: twelve thousand furlongs. Its length, breadth, and height are equal" (Revelation 21:15-16). This passage is to be connected with Ephesians 3:17-19 where Paul speaks of the length, breadth, and height of Christ's love. John sees the Lamb's wife as having the same dimensions of love as the Bridegroom—a love that is equally full and complete in length, breadth, and height.

- **Length:**
  Even as Christ's love plunged to the depths of man's sin, this bride's love reaches down to the lowest reaches of humanity to lift them up to glory. No length is spared to express the intensity of this Christlike love. She will not love her life, even unto death, for the sake of the gospel.
- **Breadth:**
  Even as Christ's love reaches across every strata and division of mankind to encompass people of every language, color, background, etc., so this love of Christ through the bride touches all peoples. Her heart is so enflamed as to embrace every person for whom Christ died.
- **Height:**
  Here are the glorious heights of her perfected love—the unspotted affections of a dazzling bride for her Beloved who is exalted above every other name. The purity and glory of her passions rise as a majestic mountain of regal splendor.

Wow, don't they make an awesome pair?! Together, clothed in stunning perfection, fully compatible and equally yoked together in every way, they are the love story of heaven. Forever.

The Secret of Clinging

I cling to Your testimonies; O LORD, do not put me to shame! (Psalm 119:31).

As "the weaker vessel," one of the things we feel deeply as the bride of Christ is our helplessness and vulnerability apart from Him. Especially in times of difficulty or trouble, when we really feel our need for Him, we will cling to Him as a person who can't swim might cling to a lifevest.

During crisis seasons, the secret place becomes our source of survival as we come aside to cling to Him and cry out for help. There are times when I'm especially clingy. I've wondered, "Lord, are you displeased that I am clinging to you so desperately right now?" The answer I've sensed is, "No, I love it when you depend on Me. Without Me you can do nothing, but you don't always own that reality. I love it when it finally sinks in that you need Me more than your very breath, and you cling to Me with all your might."

There are times when my soul is being blown about with winds, and I don't even understand the nature of the warfare. If I knew where the warfare was coming from, or if I knew how to defend myself, it would be a lot easier. But I'll find myself caught in a swirl of emotions and uncertainties, and I won't know what to do next. *The only thing I know to do in those times is to get away to the secret place, tremble before Him in my vulnerability, and cling to Him desperately.*

I used to think that Christian maturity meant that we got stronger and stronger until we were an intimidating force to be reckoned with by the powers of darkness. But the image of maturity that's given for us in Scripture is quite different from that: "Who is this coming up from the wilderness, leaning upon her beloved?" (Song of Solomon 8:5). Here we see the bride who has been perfected in love through the seasoning of the wilderness, and what quality is most striking about her? She is depending upon her Beloved for help with every step! Experience has taught her that she needs Jesus' help in literally every area of her life, so she leans on Him and clings to Him with desperate dependence.

There are many times when I get up to minister before a group of saints that I feel "wobbly." I'm groping in my spirit about how to proceed, struggling to discern the Lord's will for the ministry time at hand. I have found the stronger I feel in myself, the easier it is to move right past God. The weaker I feel, the more desperately I reach out to Him for direction and insight. Therefore, when I'm weaker, I usually follow Him more closely. So sometimes I just stand before the people and teeter. And cling to Him! As I cling to Him, I find He is amazingly faithful to direct my steps according to His will. In my times of greatest weakness I have discovered, "For by You I can run against a troop, by my God I can leap over a wall" (Psalm 18:29).

You won't mind so much clinging to Him in public if you've already been clinging to Him in private. The secret place is where we establish ourselves as clingers to His side.

When we lose our "clinginess" to Him, we become prey to all sorts of deceptions and pitfalls. Speaking of Jesus' relationship to the Jewish leaders, the Scripture says, "The stone which the builders rejected has become the chief cornerstone" (Psalm 118:22). The builders were the Jewish priests and scribes. They were schooled and trained, had done their internships, and were capable builders for God. But despite their expertise, they rejected the very stone God established as the chief cornerstone. The same temptation faces leaders today. It's possible for us, after all our training and experience, to reject the very thing God has determined to use in a central way in this hour. Attention all builders: We need to maintain a constant awareness of our own ineptitude. *Apart from a clinging relationship to the Lord, we can easily miss the stone of truth God is establishing among His people today.*

Something else I cling to in the secret place: His word. I clutch His word to my breast as though it is my very life. "I cling to Your testimonies; O LORD, do not put me to shame!" (Psalm 119:31). I think that "testimonies" point, in part, to the stories of God's mighty acts of intervention on behalf of the saints of history—how He parted the waters; how He fed them with manna; how He leveled the walls of Jericho; how He raised the dead to life. These are His testimonies, and they reflect His ways—how He handles His devout ones who love Him. I cling to the stories of God's power revealed because they encourage me that He still works in the same magnificent ways today. I cling to His testimonies for I need that same miraculous power to be released in my own life. "O LORD, do not put me to shame!"

After Jesus rose from the dead, He appeared first to Mary Magdalene (intentionally so). You see, Mary was the last one at the tomb on the day of His burial, and she was the first one at the tomb on the morning of the third day. When nobody else was there, Mary was. So Jesus revealed Himself first to the one who loved and missed Him most! When Mary saw Him, she was overcome with joy, and wrapped her arms around his feet. Jesus said to her, "'Do not cling to Me, for I have not yet ascended to My Father'" (John 20:17). He was not rebuking her as though He thought she shouldn't have clung to Him like that. He was simply meaning, "It's not time yet. I know the purity of your heart, Mary, that you long to be joined in love to Me. But I have to ascend to the Father first before we cling to each other in the kingdom of God."

In clinging to Jesus, Mary Magdalene was a representation of the endtime bride of Christ. Like Mary of long ago, there is a bridal company today that is yearning for His appearing, looking for Him, peering into the darkness, lovesick with longing to see Him. Weeping. And waiting. This is the kind of bride Jesus is coming back for. And when He reveals Himself to her the second time, she will not be put off any longer. Even if He should try to say, "Don't cling to Me," these arms will wrap around His feet, and I'll never let go! "We lost you once, Lord, and I'm never letting you out of my grip ever again!" And so we will cling to Him forever in love.

But until that glorious day, I will cling to Him in secret, and there I will give Him my love.

48

The Secret of Walking With God

God is looking for not only a clinging bride but also a walking partner. From the very beginning, God had a relationship with Adam and Eve that found them "walking in the garden in the cool of the day" (Genesis 3:8). God created man for the enjoyment of a walking relationship that involved companionship, dialogue, intimacy, joint decision-making, mutual delight, and shared dominion. God longs to walk with you, which is why His arms of grace have been pulling you into a closer walk with Him.

My wife, Marci, loves to go walking with her friend, Wendy. They talk the whole time. Nonstop. The walk not only makes exercise fun, it also deepens their friendship. Jesus went on these kinds of walks with His disciples, and He still likes to walk with us this way today.

The secret place is not the destination; it is only the catalyst. It is designed of God to establish us in an intimate friendship with Him that is walked out through the course of our everyday lives. *The goal we're after is an everyday walk of unbroken communion with our Lord and Friend.*

Enoch was the first man in the Bible who walked with God:

> After he begot Methuselah, *Enoch walked with God* three hundred years, and had sons and daughters. So all the days of Enoch were three hundred and sixty-five years. And *Enoch walked with God*; and he was not, for God took him" (Genesis 5:22-24).

Even though men began to call upon the name of the Lord in the early days (Genesis 4:26), Enoch was the first man to uncover the true delight of walking with God. He found something even Adam didn't experience. He pressed into God until he learned how to commune with God through every facet of life. To find that dimension of relationship certainly required an intense spiritual pursuit, and then when he found it the Lord made a graphic statement by catching him up to heaven.

By taking Enoch up to glory, God wasn't trying to get us impressed with Enoch's piety. Nor was God saying, "If you get to be as spiritual as Enoch, you'll get translated up to heaven, too." This was a unique experience God used to emphasize a specific point. God's point was, *"I love to walk with man! Enoch was the first man to truly walk with Me, so I decided to highlight His example by doing something extraordinary with him. I took Him up to paradise to underscore how much I value and desire a daily walking relationship with My chosen ones."* Enoch's example continues to witness to all generations of the great zeal God has to walk with man.

When the zeal of God captures you, it will ignite you with a great passion to walk with God and to be His friend. Imagine being Enoch and living 365 years—and having this growing relationship with God! One can only wonder what glorious depths of intimacy Enoch uncovered. Perhaps Enoch's heart longed so deeply for more of God that God grew weary of withholding Himself. Maybe God's heart was saying, "Enoch, you love Me with such a pure and sweet passion, I don't want to say 'no' to you anymore. I'm going to answer your prayer and show you My face. Come on up!"

As you draw close to God, He will not likely take you up to heaven as He did Enoch. However, He does desire to reveal the beauty of His face to you. As we walk with Him, He will open the Scriptures to us through the Spirit of wisdom and revelation and reveal to us the light of the glory of God that is to be found in Him.

There was one other aspect of Enoch's ascension that is significant. God waited until Enoch was 365 years old—and then poof, he was gone. Since there are 365 days in a year, Enoch's life span of 365 years was in itself a message from God. God was basically saying, "I want to walk with man 365 days a year. 364 days a year won't do. I want to walk with you today, all day, every day, all year long, for the rest of your earthly lifetime!" Wow, it's mindboggling to consider that the great God of the universe is so intensely interested in *us*!

When we walk with God, we enter the dimension where God unfolds the secrets of His kingdom. These are the paths that the ancients trod before us. Noah knew the secret of walking with God (Genesis 6:9), as did Abraham (Genesis 24:40). Through Christ, you can explore the glorious riches of knowing God like they did—and to even a greater degree because of the Spirit which has been given to us!

God wants to walk *with* us before He works *through* us. So He will wait to act until He finds the right man or woman through whom He can work. To put it bluntly, God works with His friends. He doesn't decide what He wants to do and then start looking for someone to use. He looks for a man or a woman, and once He finds him or her, He then decides what He wants to do with them. For example, God didn't choose Noah because He wanted to send a flood; God had the freedom to send a flood because He had found a man to walk with. God always starts by finding a friend first.

When God has a Noah, He can do a flood. When God has a Joseph, He can give Pharaoh a divine dream. When God has a Moses, He can plan a mighty deliverance for His people. When God has an Elijah, He can send fire from heaven. When God has a Samuel, He can test Saul's heart. When God has a Jesus, He can save the world. Oh beloved, learn to walk with God!

When God has a friend, divine activity accelerates. Things were fairly regular around Babylon until Daniel showed up. But now that there was a man in Babylon who walked with God, God could accelerate His purposes. All kinds of things started to happen. Nebuchadnezzar began to receive divine dreams; men were preserved in a fiery furnace; Nebuchadnezzar lost his mind for seven years and then was restored; a hand appeared and wrote on a wall; Daniel was delivered from the mouth of the lions; and some of the most detailed revelations of future events were recorded. All these things could take place because God had a Daniel who walked with Him.

When God has a useful vessel that has been prepared for noble purposes, He *will* use that vessel. To illustrate, if you put a riding lawn mower in my garage, I promise you this—I *will* use it! Similarly, God will use the one who walks with Him. But He's looking especially for three crucial qualities: humility, faithfulness, and loyalty. He wants to work with friends who are loyal to Him, no matter what. Even when circumstances would suggest God is unjust, His true friends continue to walk with Him. So the Lord will test our fidelity. When we prove ourselves His friends through the greatest calamities of life, we qualify as useful vessels.

Jesus was the quintessential example of a Man who walked with God. He walked so closely with God that He was always in the Spirit, even when shaking Himself awake from a groggy sleep. When I first wake up, I'm sometimes grumpy or dopey. But when they awakened Jesus out of a deep sleep, He silenced the storm! What an amazing attainment, to be awakened out of a dead sleep and be instantly in the Spirit. Lord, if I should awake in this Your likeness, with this depth of walk, then I shall be satisfied!

Here's the secret: *The secret place is where we develop a walking relationship with God.* We must develop a secret history with God before He gives us a public history before people. Hidden in the secret place, we learn what He's looking for in friends, and we find out what pleases Him. Our inner chamber with Him becomes our training ground for a life that is rooted and grounded in love.

Jesus told us that He confides His kingdom purposes to His friends (John 15:15). Lord, I want to be Your friend, your confidant, loyal to the death. I want to walk with You, talk with You, listen to You, hear Your heart, and participate in Your activities in this momentous hour. Teach me, Lord, to walk with You!

49

The Secret of Buying Oil

Oil in the Bible is often representative of the Holy Spirit, so to have oil in our lamps means to have the indwelling presence of the Holy Spirit illuminating our lives with His zeal and glory. Without the oil of the Holy Spirit, our lives become lifeless, and our light is extinguished. The secret place is where we buy oil. As we come aside to commune with our Lord, we are renewed in the Holy Spirit, and our oil levels are replenished.

The idea of "buying oil" derives from the parable of the ten virgins, so let's look at that passage and take special note of how the word "oil" appears in the parable. Jesus is speaking:

> "Then the kingdom of heaven shall be likened to ten virgins who took their lamps and went out to meet the bridegroom. Now five of them were wise, and five were foolish. Those who were foolish took their lamps and took no oil with them, but the wise took oil in their vessels with their lamps. But while the bridegroom was delayed, they all slumbered and slept. And at midnight a cry was heard: 'Behold, the bridegroom is coming; go out to meet him!' Then all those virgins arose and trimmed their lamps. And the foolish said to the wise, 'Give us

some of your oil, for our lamps are going out.' But the wise answered, saying, 'No, lest there should not be enough for us and you; but go rather to those who sell, and buy for yourselves.' And while they went to buy, the bridegroom came, and those who were ready went in with him to the wedding; and the door was shut. Afterward the other virgins came also, saying, 'Lord, Lord, open to us!' But he answered and said, 'Assuredly, I say to you, I do not know you.' Watch therefore, for you know neither the day nor the hour in which the Son of Man is coming" (Matthew 25:1-13).

We do not have space in this brief chapter for a thorough study of this parable. This is an incredibly fascinating parable, and it has earned a wide variety of interpretations and applications. However, the vast majority would agree that oil in the lamp represents having an inner reservoir of Holy Spirit reality. Our focus here is on the oil. If we are not filled with the oil of the Spirit, we will not survive the chaos and calamities of the last days.

All ten virgins had oil in their lamps, but the five wise virgins brought an extra vessel of oil with them. This was because the wise virgins had anticipated that the return of the bridegroom might possibly be delayed beyond their expectations. The foolish virgins made the fatal assumption the bridegroom's return would be sooner than later. They were confident that they didn't need extra oil; they thought their lamp held enough oil to sustain them until the bridegroom's coming.

All ten were virgins, which is to say they were all sincere believers. Mike Bickle has suggested, based on the context, that the virgins represent leaders in the church. If that's true, then the oil could be said to represent a leader's ministry anointing that is cultivated in the secret place. The foolish virgins had a "get by" mentality. They invested themselves in the secret place only to the degree that their ministry responsibilities seemed to dictate. The wise showed their diligence by garnering a depth in God that was greater than their present ministries demanded of them. *The wise did not come to the secret place simply to buy oil*

for ministry impartation; they also came to buy oil for them-
selves in order to have a private burning-heart relationship with
the Lord.

It doesn't cost much to get oil for ministry, but it will cost
you a lot to get the oil of an intimate relationship with Jesus.
Then, when the ministry time is over, you're still a burning love-
flame for Him.

The oil of authentic relationship is bought at the cost of investing time and energy in the secret place. The foolish will allow
urgent matters of the moment to pull them away from the secret
place after having a minimal filling. The wise will stay and continue to be filled with oil until their hearts are energized by their
love relationship with Jesus.

When their foolishness becomes obvious, the foolish will turn
to the wise and say, "Give us some of your oil." They will recognize the wise have a depth in God that they never took the time
and energy to cultivate. They will say, "Give us some of your authority in ministry," but the wise will understand that there are
no shortcuts to ministry authority. *You can't derive the author-*
ity of anointing from another person; you have to get it yourself
in the secret place.

When the bridegroom delays His return, the virgins are over-
taken with heartsickness because of deferred hope (Proverbs
13:12). Heartsickness will cause them to sleep from sorrow (Luke
22:45). The bridegroom's delay has a way of distinguishing between the foolish and the wise. It reveals those who had developed their own personal history of a living relationship with the
bridegroom. Those who persevere in love through the heartsickness of deferred hopes will be entrusted with the authority to
minister deliverance to the captives. The wise will become mighty
deliverers in the end.

We will need a reservoir in the Spirit if we are to sustain
through the hour of trial that is to come upon the entire earth
(Revelation 3:10). The point of the parable is—buy oil! Devote
yourself to the secret place until your heart is overflowing with
love and zeal for your Beloved. Then, make it the first priority of

your day to keep that oil replenished. The secret is right here: *The secret place is the threshold for resourcing the replenishment you need to sustain through the dark night of Christ's delays.*

Buy oil!

50

The Secret of Constant Supply

God has made available the opportunity to tap into a cease less supply of the Spirit. We don't ever have to become depleted spiritually, if we could but learn to access the constant supply of the indwelling Spirit. In the secret place, we enlarge our capacity to draw upon His grace, and then we live out our days in the strength of His eternal resources.

The imagery of "constant supply" is painted most vividly in Zechariah 4. Please open your Bible to Zechariah 4 right now, and read it first before moving ahead with me.

Zechariah was shown a lampstand with seven oil-fed lamps on it. He saw a bowl full of oil above the lampstand, with pipes feeding down from the bowl into each lamp. The bowl acted as a reservoir of oil, and was itself fed by two olive trees which stood on the left and right of the lampstand. The olive trees dripped oil constantly into two receptacles, which fed the oil down into the bowl. The trees fed the bowl; the bowl fed the lamps. The supply was constant, and the fires in the lamps burned without cessation.

What I am about to share is not the only way to view Zechariah 4. There are many valid interpretations for prophetic passages such as this, and so my interpretation is only one among several possible interpretations. With that disclaimer, I would like to suggest the lampstand represents *you*—the devoted servant of the Lord. In the context of Zechariah 4, the lampstand is Zerubbabel, but Zerubbabel only typifies the devoted servant of the Lord. Lampstands in the Bible represent various things, but in Matthew 5:15 Jesus used a lampstand to refer to an individual. So the lampstand is you, the individual believer.

At first I didn't see the lampstand as representing an individual because I thought an individual believer had only one fire burning within. But then I came across Jesus' exhortation, "'Let your waist be girded and your lamps burning'" (Luke 12:25). We have one waist, so waist is singular. But Jesus put "lamps" in the plural, saying that we have multiple lamps within us. We have more than one lamp burning within our hearts—we have *seven*, to be precise. God designs that each of us burn with seven holy fires before the presence of His glory. The Holy Spirit is revealed as "seven lamps of fire" that burn before the throne (Revelation 4:5). When you are filled with the Holy Spirit, you too will burn with seven fires. I am unprepared to make a statement on what I think those seven fires are, but I think the foremost lamp is the fire of God's love. It is the burning love of God for God and for His creation. When that fire grips our lives, it sets us ablaze with fiery passion for Jesus and merciful compassion for people. And that's just one of the seven fires. (I am peering into the other six fires, and may write on that someday.)

Now let's look at the historical background to Zechariah's vision. Zerubbabel, Israel's civic leader, is involved in the task of building the temple of God. The prophet Zechariah, his court counselor, is given a divine message to encourage Zerubbabel in his building project. God wants to reveal to Zerubbabel a totally new paradigm for building in the kingdom. Most kingdom building is done by visionary leaders who mobilize a group of people to draw upon their strengths and hammer away at the project with all their might until it's finished. Zechariah has a divine revelation, however, into another kind of leadership—a style of leadership in which the servant of the Lord derives his effectiveness by drawing upon an inner source in the Spirit. As he is fed on the inside by a constant supply of the Spirit, the leader is empowered to lead God's people in the building of the kingdom. *Instead of seeing a leader who is spread thin by running in a thousand directions at once, Zechariah sees a leader whose lamps are burning brightly because he is drawing upon a spiritual lifesource of power and grace.* "'"Not by might nor by power, but by My Spirit," says the LORD of hosts'" (Zechariah 4:6).

It's interesting that the storage bowl, which is full of oil, is said to be "above" the lampstand. This means that the oil pours *down* from the bowl into the seven lamps. Not only does this bowl contain more than enough oil to sustain the lamps, it also supplies each of the lamps with *gravity-fed pressure*. With the oil pressing down eagerly into each flame, the lamps are not flickering lazily but they are burning fiercely and brightly—veritable torches of divine zeal. God is showing Zechariah that it's possible to access such a dynamic flow of divine life that one literally burns with holy zeal before God's throne and before people on earth.

Let's stop and make this personal and practical. See yourself as this lampstand, as a devout believer who is called to provide compassionate leadership in the building of the kingdom of God. As you come aside into the secret place, you open the channels of your heart and allow the oil of divine life to flow into every chamber of your heart. The secret place is where your lamps are trimmed and where your zeal for the face of Christ is rekindled and renewed until you burn with seven bright, fiery, torch-like flames. Those who come into contact with you are impacted with your passion for Jesus and your selfless love for people. They realize you've been seared clean from self-serving ambitions and personal agendas. Your fire is hot and your flame is pure. Your heart is enthralled with the beauty of your King. Your interests and affections are for nothing other than your heavenly Bridegroom. When you sound a call to build, the saints rally around you enthusiastically because they know you're functioning from the creative womb of the morning (the secret place) where you've received divinely downloaded mandates and insights. Your productivity becomes disproportionate to your resources. What I mean is, the work accelerates forward at a pace that is faster than seems possible with the limited resources at your disposal. Why? *Because you're not just working by the might and power of human resources; you're operating in the synergy and flow of Holy Spirit momentum as God Himself works with you and in you. You've found the God zone!* Financial resources come out of seemingly nowhere; volunteers come out of the proverbial woodwork; heathen corporations start donating their stuff to you; doors open where only a wall existed; saints are joined together in kingdom purpose; sinners are in awe of the grace of God that rests upon the community of believers. And it was all unlocked because a servant leader came out of the secret place on fire for God!

Now back to the vision of Zechariah 4. Zechariah has one consuming question of the angel who is bringing him this revelation. Zechariah asks the angel no less than three times, "Tell me about those two olive trees. What are the olive trees?" (See verses 4, 11, and 12.) The angel's answer is, "'These are the two anointed ones, who stand beside the Lord of the whole earth'" (Zechariah 4:14). That answer is vague enough that we still find ourselves asking the question, what do these two olive trees represent?

Zechariah wants to know what the two olive trees are because they are the source of the oil. Once we know the source, we know the secret to living in a constant supply of divine life and grace. So this really is the great question of all time. What is the source for a never-ending supply of God's infinite resources?

The two olive trees, in my judgment, are the word and the Spirit. We need both the word and Spirit, mixed together and flowing into our spirits, if we are to build the kingdom through the power of God. When the Spirit of God moves upon His word and speaks it into the depths of your being, you will come alive with a holy fire! That's why when Jesus revealed Jesus to the two disciples on the road to Emmaus, opening the Scriptures regarding Himself to their heart through the power of the Holy Spirit, those disciples later declared, "'Did not our heart burn within us while He talked with us on the road, and while He opened the Scriptures to us?'" (Luke 24:32). *When the Spirit-empowered word is ministered to your heart, you too will burn for Him!*

The secret place is where we draw upon the life of the word and the Spirit. It's the place where we open our spirits to Him so that a greater flow of His oil might make its way to our lamps. What we really want is *wider pipes*. The pipes that carry the oil from the bowl to the seven lamps are critical to the degree of light emitted by the lampstand. If the pipes are open and un-clogged, oil will flow freely to the flames of our hearts. When this admixture of oil (the word and the Spirit) flows into our hearts and sets us ablaze for Him, the kingdom will advance in and through our lives in staggering proportions. The issue is not, "Work harder!" The issue is, "Get oil!" The secret is: Apply your-self to enlarging your connection to the source of divine oil. The more this oil flows into your inner being, the brighter your lamps will blaze before God and men.

Nothing is more dangerous to the kingdom of darkness than a man or woman who has found the unceasing wellspring of heaven's life. When the servant of the Lord is fed from this inner flow of oil and his seven lamps are veritable torches of flaming zeal for his Beloved, then no force of hell can extinguish this flame. Even if hell tries to douse this flame with the floods of the dragon's mouth, this fire is fed by an internal source. Nothing external can quench it. Oh what a marvelous secret I am trying to describe! John Wesley said it something like this, "Get on fire for God and let people come and watch you burn."

Come with me to the next chapter, I want to emphasize this truth with yet another scriptural image that portrays a constant supply of divine life.

51

The Secret of Abiding In Christ

There is a huge question that has been asked by all of the greatest saints throughout history in their pursuit of God. We saw in our previous chapter that this question was asked three times by Zechariah. It is the common quest of the diligent soul. It is the shared question of all generations, for all time. The question is very simply, "How do I abide in Christ?" The question is simple, but the answer profound. And few there be that find it.

Many of us feel like we move in and out of God's throneroom. We have times of great connectedness, and then we suffer periods of disconnectedness. We can't always analyze exactly why a distance has developed in our hearts toward the Lord, but most of us feel like our relationship with Christ is a roller coaster ride of feeling close, then far, then close, then far, then close again. In and out. And we hate it. We were created for constant intimacy, and anything less drives us crazy on the inside.

In my opinion, these are some of the most glorious words of Christ in the entire Bible: "'If you abide in Me, and My words abide in you, you will ask what you desire, and it shall be done for you. By this My Father is glorified, that you bear much fruit; so you will be My disciples'" (John 15:7-8). The "if" of the passage almost drives me insane with holy desire. "If!" The great condition to answered prayer is an abiding relationship with Christ and His words. This attainment is not guaranteed. It is available, but rarely experienced in fullness. I know that I do not abide in Christ in this way because the things I desire are not yet done for me. So I seek this dimension of holy living with great spiritual appetite—with what I call "holy heartburn." I must gain Christ!

A Christian magazine that featured Hudson Taylor in one of its issues referred to how Taylor struggled for a closer walk with God. Although he is considered one of the greatest missionary champions of church history, he longed for a more intimate relationship with Christ. "I prayed, agonized, fasted, strove, made resolutions, read the word more diligently, sought more time for retirement and meditation—but all was without effect," he pined. "I knew that if I would abide in Christ all would be well, but I could not." Taylor reached a turning point in his life when he received a letter from a colleague. This simple message unlocked the door: "Friendship with God comes not from striving after faith but from resting in the faithful one." Those simple words were somehow precisely what Hudson Taylor needed to help him cross a threshold in his relationship with Christ. He was able to cease striving and to embrace Christ's nearness and power and life. I refer to Taylor's experience, not as though it's a formula for learning to abide in Christ, but rather to show that the most eminent of saints have wrestled with this very issue.

How you come to abide in Christ will be different from all others. We all abide differently because we are all unique creations of God. Your relationship with Christ will never be like mine, and mine will never be like yours. That's why you'll never learn to abide in Christ by reading the stories of others. You won't learn to abide by reading the right book or listening to a great sermon. No one can mentor you into an abiding relationship with Christ. A mentor might be able to help to a limited degree, but in the final analysis we all have to find our own way to abiding in Christ. *When all is said and done, we must shut the door, get into the secret place with God, and discover what an abiding relationship with Christ will look like for ourselves.*

Usually the pathway to an abiding relationship with Christ is attended with duress. God allows uncomfortable circumstances or emotions in our lives that press us into Christ with vigilant determination. Most of us will never abandon ourselves to pursuing an abiding relationship unless the Lord, in His kindness, allows calamities or struggles in our lives that elevate our pain level to the point of desperation.

Joseph illustrates this truth quintessentially. God took Joseph on a painful pathway in order to help him find an abiding relationship. Let me review the story very briefly with you.

As a 17-year-old, Joseph stood apart from his brothers as a man of godly character in the midst of a perverse generation. So God basically said, "Congratulations, Joseph, you're keeping your heart pure; you're walking blamelessly before God and man; you're keeping yourself separate from an evil generation. You've qualified for a promotion in the kingdom—to slavery you go!" So Joseph was sold into slavery by his brothers.

In Egypt, he was sold to a man named Potiphar. Potiphar soon realized God was with Joseph and that He blessed everything Joseph touched. So Potiphar made Joseph the chief steward of all his possessions. Although a slave, Joseph kept his heart before God and continued to walk carefully before God. He was diligent to cultivate his gifts and talents, proving himself faithful as a steward over the house. He fled from sexual temptation when Potiphar's wife tried to seduce him. So God responded, "Congratulations, Joseph, you're continuing to practice my presence; you're faithfully cultivating your gifts and talents; and you're fleeing temptation. You've qualified for another promotion in the kingdom—to prison you go!"

Joseph had no idea why he was in prison. Surely he must have been tempted with the thought, "God, what is the use of serving You? When I love You and serve You and keep a guard upon my heart, it does me no good." Satan wanted to convince Joseph that serving God didn't pay. But Joseph chose to push away the tempter's thoughts, and instead he set his love upon God even in the prison. He held to the dreams God had given him of eventual promotion.

However, a desperation took hold of Joseph's spirit. Joseph realized that apart from divine intervention, he would spend the rest of his life rotting in this Egyptian prison. None of his talents would work for him here. It didn't matter that he was gifted and charismatic and intelligent; none of those things could get him out of prison. Every gift he had cultivated was now useless. Reduced to total helplessness, Joseph began to cry out to God with intense desperation. "God, talk to me, or my life is over!" He began to push down roots into the Spirit of God, deeper than ever before. "God, why have you allowed this to happen to me?"

God said, "Deeper." So he put the roots down deeper. "Still deeper." So in his desperation, Joseph pressed into the depths of the Spirit of God. "Deeper, Joseph."

Joseph kept sinking his spiritual roots deeper and deeper into the Spirit of God—until one day he found the river! There is a river, dear friend, that makes glad the city of God. This subterranean river runs so deep that most don't find it. But in some cases God will allow extreme duress to press His servant into the depths of the Spirit with an unprecedented passion. When Joseph found this river, he found a lifesource in God that goes deeper than the seasons of life. *Whether it's flood season or drought season, there is a river available to the saint providing a constant source of divine life and Spirit empowerment. Very few seem to find this great underground river, but when you find it, it is called "abiding in Christ."*

God was saying to Joseph, "Son, I have a great promotion in store for you. But what I'm calling you to will never be managed on the strength of your giftings and talents. And I know that as long as your strengths are intact, you will always default to them. So I'm going to put you in a place where your strengths will be useless. I'm putting you in prison! In the helplessness of losing all control, you will have to find a dimension in Me that supercedes your gifts and talents. You see, Joseph, there is a dimension in Me that is not of your might and power, but it is by My Spirit." When Joseph found that river, it was his ability to draw upon the life of God that lifted him from the prison. It wasn't his talents that delivered him from prison, but his life in the Spirit. When

211

Pharaoh called upon Joseph to interpret his dream, Joseph was able to tap into the river and give Pharaoh the wisdom that he desired. And in one day, Joseph went from the prison to the palace!

It is an abiding relationship with Christ that launches the saint into the God zone. I'm talking about the dimension where God works sovereignly and mightily in the affairs of men. Jesus had an abiding relationship with His Father, and He changed the history of our planet. *If God will grant you the grace to find this never-ending source of divine power called "abiding in Christ," then you will change your generation for God as well!*

Do not be discouraged by the duress and hardship that has suddenly come upon you. Press into God like you never have in all your life! Allow the desperation of your soul to help you pursue God with absolute abandonment. The secret is this: If you will seek Him with all your heart, He will guide you to the ancient river that runs deep in the heart of God. As you chase Him with every ounce of your strength, He will bring you to the fountain of divine life. When the life of God begins to flow into your world of impossibilities, this is the stuff of miracles. The life of God cannot be stopped! If you drink of this river, everything in you and around you will begin to shake and shudder under the groundswell of God's power released. Everything about your prison is about to change! I pray you might receive this word: *Learn to abide in Christ!*

52

The Secret of Union With God

There is a profound cry, deep in the heart of man, for a heart connection with God. You were created to abide in Christ! It is this cry for intimacy with God that has driven you to read this book. It was that same cry for a connection with God that filled the heart of the Samaritan woman in John 4, even though she didn't even know how to articulate her longings. She had looked for love in all the wrong places, but the Master saw her heart and He knew how to draw it out.

When Jesus spoke with this woman at Jacob's well and she realized that Jesus was a prophet, she immediately put forward her number one question: "'Our fathers worshiped on this mountain, and you Jews say that in Jerusalem is the place where one ought to worship'" (John 4:20). Her question was, "What's the right way to connect with God—here on this mountain or in Jerusalem?" Above all else, the longing of her heart was for a meaningful connection with God's heart. The issue of "where" had been argued so much in her day that she had despaired of ever connecting with God, and had succumbed to a lifestyle of flagrant sin. But despite her sinful lifestyle and sense of hopelessness at ever finding it, her heart still ached for a connection with God! Jesus' response must have amazed her. She learned even

213

though she was seeking to connect with God, God was even more actively interested in seeking those who would connect with Him in Spirit and in truth (John 4:23). Jesus sought her out to reveal to her the Father's desire for worshipers like *her!*

God has shown Himself to be so much different from what we would have thought. He longs for us, to be one with us, to have one heartbeat with us. The ancients had a term to describe these higher dimensions of spiritual intimacy, which they called "union with God." This is the connection with God for which the human heart burns. Jesus came to make us one with God (John 17:21-23). *It is in union with God that we find the greatest exhilaration, and it is also where we discover the most glorious enticements to explore the cavernous depths of God's burning heart.*

God breathed into the human soul a profound desire for union with Him. Then, He equipped us with the vocabulary to talk about it when He gave us the model of marriage. He said, "Therefore a man shall leave his father and mother and be joined to his wife, and they shall become one flesh" (Genesis 2:24). The union of marriage was to serve as an example that would give us a mental template for understanding spiritual union.

Now, why do a young man and woman choose to get married? Is it for romance? Well, a couple can enjoy romance within courtship without getting married. They can have love, intimacy, friendship, companionship, communication, fellowship—all those things—and still not get married. (I am speaking of courtship in its purity and innocence.) So why get married? Because while a couple can enjoy all the above benefits of relating to one another in purity and integrity without getting married, there's one thing they can't have. Couples get married, essentially, for *union.*

God has given us a great desire for union—with our spouse, and even moreso with Him. *We know there is a day coming in which we will be joined to Christ at the marriage supper of the Lamb, but the Scripture has clearly shown that there are dimensions of union with Christ that are available to us in the here and now.* The fullness is coming later, but what is available to us now is deserving of our diligent pursuit.

There is one verse, above all others, that has drawn me into the pursuit of union with God. It is tucked away in such an obscure way that I had moved right past the verse many times before. But one day the verse snagged me: "But he who is joined to the Lord is one spirit with Him" (1 Corinthians 6:17). In context, Paul is speaking of the union that happens through sexual relations. His inference is that the sexual union is somehow pointing to a kind of spiritual union that we have with Christ which far supercedes the physical/sexual plane.

Here's what grabbed me about the verse. It says the Lord and I are *one spirit*. When I envisioned spiritual communion with the Lord, I always envisioned two separate spirits, as though His Spirit and mine were kissing. But this Scripture reveals that when we're joined to Christ, we are no longer two spirits but one. *One spirit with God!* The idea is so fantastic as to almost appear preposterous or absurd. *When I surrender to Christ, we two become one.*

Christ in me, the hope of glory! The highest heavens and the earth cannot contain God (Acts 7:49-50), but somehow God has created the human soul with the ability to be a habitation for Himself. There is something within us that is broader in its ability to contain God than the universe. This is the wonder of what God has made us to be. I can "be filled with all the fullness of God" (Ephesians 3:19), with the fullness of "Him who fills all in all" (Ephesians 1:23). The highest heavens can't contain God, but the human spirit can. Wow!

Let me illustrate this with a question. If I were to pour a cup of pure water into the ocean, would you say the ocean is now diluted? No, you would say that cup of pure water has been totally absorbed and lost in the vastness of the ocean. That's what happens in union with Christ. *When I am joined to Him, I lose my identity in the ocean of His greatness, so that now I can say, "It is no longer I who live, but Christ lives in me" (Galatians 2:20).* I am one with Him, and my identity is gloriously lost in the immensity of His majesty and splendor.

Do not take me to mean that we become God. Far from it. We are eternally the created, and He is eternally the Creator. The chasm between Creator and created will remain forever. But in some glorious way, the created becomes one spirit with the Creator, joined together in eternal affections of love and devotion.

If this thought seems mindboggling to you, it has the angels absolutely dumbfounded. From eternity past, there is a fiery furnace of love that has been limited to but Three. The Father, Son, and Holy Ghost have enjoyed an affection of astronomical proportions that is so fiery in its intensity and scope that no other creature would even dare step into this blazing furnace of divine love. Oh the love that draws the Father into the heart of the Son, and the Spirit into the heart of the Father, and the Son into the heart of the Spirit! And now, as the angels gaze into this blazing inferno, they see the form of a fourth walking in the midst of the fire. And this fourth person has the appearance of the bride of Christ! Fallen mankind has been elevated to oneness with the Godhead! The ramifications are beyond comprehension to even the brilliant ones who blaze before God's throne.

We are one spirit with God! And all that's required is that we be "joined to Christ." But what does it mean to be joined to Christ?

The Old Testament word for "joined" has a variety of colorings in its meaning. One fascinating sense of the word is found in Psalm 63:8, "My soul *follows close* behind You." The original word for "follows close" is related to the word "joined." So the idea of the word literally is, "to pursue with the intent to overtake." David is saying, "Lord, I am pursuing very closely behind You, and I am determined to overtake You. And when I do, I will lay hold of You and will never let You go! I will be joined to You forever!"

So to be joined to Christ is to chase Him with abandoned intensity—to pursue Him with the intent of laying hold of Him. This is the holy chase to which we've been invited, and it is the magnificent obsession of the secret place.

When I think of being joined to Christ and how I might illustrate that truth for you, I am drawn to the example of Mary Magdalene. Mary Magdalene represents the endtime bride of Christ who is pursuing Christ with the desire of being joined to Him. Christ had cast seven demons out of her, and because she had been forgiven much she loved much. That love was evidenced in the way she wept at Jesus' tomb and was the first one to seek

Him on resurrection morning. Mary had taken up the holy chase, so when Jesus revealed Himself to her she instantly wrapped her arms around Jesus' feet. Her heart craved union with God.

Like Mary, the bride of Christ stands today, at the end of the ages, looking with longing for the appearing of her Lord. "Heavenly Father, where have You carried Him away? Bring Him to me, and I will draw away with Him, for I long to be with Him." And so like Mary at the tomb, we are looking, weeping, longing, yearning, watching. Surely He is coming back to reveal Himself first to this bride who longs for Him most! And when He comes this second time, we will have found the one for whom our soul longs. Our pursuit will be ended, for we will overtake our Beloved, lay hold of Him, and never let go.

In that moment He "will transform our lowly body that it may be conformed to His glorious body" (Philippians 3:21). This heavenly Bride and Groom will walk the aisle of Glory together, and be joined together in holy matrimony under the officiating ministry of the Father of lights. Nothing will ever separate us again. There will be no more crying, no more pain, no more tears. The Desire of the Nations will be fulfilled. And so we will ever be with the Lord!

But until then, I will retreat to my secret place, a heartsick, lovesick bride who longs to behold her Bridegroom. I will pursue Him with the intent of overtaking Him. And I will exult in our quiet secret—the place of highest intimacy—for here I am joined to Him and we are one spirit.

Description of Resources on the Facing Page

❖ THE FIRE OF GOD'S LOVE compels us toward the passionate love that God is producing within the bride in this hour for her Bridegroom, the Lord Jesus.

❖ GLORY: WHEN HEAVEN INVADES EARTH articulates the highest goal of worship—to behold the Glory of God! Be renewed in the assurance that God's Glory is coming, and let your vision be kindled for a personal, life-changing encounter with God Himself.

❖ PAIN, PERPLEXITY & PROMOTION looks at the book of Job from a fresh, prophetic vantage. Job's life shows how God promotes His chosen vessels to higher heights than they would have conceived possible. Let Job's example compel you toward God's highest and best!

❖ THE FIRE OF DELAYED ANSWERS explores how God sometimes delays the answers to our prayers in order to produce godly character in us. This book is "spiritual food" for those in crisis or difficulty.

❖ IN HIS FACE propels the reader passionately toward a more personal and intimate relationship with Jesus Christ. Challenging devotional reading.

❖ EXPLORING WORSHIP is a 300-page textbook that covers a full range of subjects related to praise and worship. Translated into several languages, this bestselling book is being used internationally as a text by many Bible colleges, Bible study groups, and worship leading teams. Also available is an accompanying WORKBOOK/DISCUSSION GUIDE.

❖ DEALING WITH THE REJECTION AND PRAISE OF MAN is a booklet that shows how to hold your heart before God in a way that pleases Him in the midst of both rejection and praise from people.

Order Form

Books by Bob Sorge

	Qty.	Price	Total
BOOKS:			
SECRETS OF THE SECRET PLACE	____	$12.00	____
GLORY: When Heaven Invades Earth	____	$ 8.00	____
PAIN, PERPLEXITY & PROMOTION	____	$12.00	____
THE FIRE OF GOD'S LOVE	____	$12.00	____
THE FIRE OF DELAYED ANSWERS	____	$12.00	____
IN HIS FACE: A Prophetic Call to Renewed Focus	____	$11.00	____
EXPLORING WORSHIP: A Practical Guide to Praise and Worship	____	$13.00	____
Exploring Worship WORKBOOK & DISCUSSION GUIDE	____	$ 5.00	____
DEALING WITH THE REJECTION AND PRAISE OF MAN	____	$ 8.00	____
SPECIAL PACKET #2			
One of each book	____	$65.00	____
(Special Packet Includes Free Shipping)			

Subtotal	____
Shipping, Add 10% (Minimum of $2.00)	____
Missouri Residents Add 7.475% Sales Tax	____
Total Enclosed	____

U.S. Funds Only

Send payment with order to: Oasis House
P.O. Box 127
Greenwood, MO 64034-0127

Name _____

Address: Street _____

City _____ State _____

Zip _____

For MasterCard/VISA orders and quantity discounts,
call 816-623-9050

Or order on our fully secure website:
www.oasishouse.net